THE VEGETARIAN'S COMPLETE
QUINOA COOKBOOK

THE VEGETARIAN'S COMPLETE
QUINOA COOKBOOK

edited by Mairlyn Smith, PHEc   from the Ontario Home Economics Association

whitecap

WHITECAP BOOKS

Whitecap Books is known for its expertise in the cookbook
market and has produced some of the most innovative and
familiar titles found in kitchens across North America.

PUBLISHER: Michael Burch
EDITORS: Naomi Pauls and Theresa Best
DESIGNER: Diane (Yee) Robertson
FOOD PHOTOGRAPHY: Mike McColl
FOOD STYLING: Joan Ttooulias, PHEc

The following recipes appear in other publications and have
been used with permission: Gluten-Free Ancient Grains
Bread (Mixer Method), *Complete Gluten-Free Cookbook*
(Robert Rose, 2007); Gluten-Free Ancient Grains Bread
(Bread Machine Method), *125 Best Gluten-Free Bread
Machine Recipes* (Robert Rose, 2010); Historic Grains Bread,
300 Best Canadian Bread Machine Recipes (Robert Rose,
2010); Pecan and Quinoa–Stuffed Squash, *250 Gluten-Free
Favorites* (Robert Rose, 2009); Gluten-Free Quinoa Flax
Cookies, Baked Custard, *The Gluten-Free Baking Book*
(Robert Rose, 2011).

Printed in Canada

LIBRARY AND ARCHIVES CANADA CATALOGUING
IN PUBLICATION

Ontario Home Economics Association

The vegetarian's complete quinoa cookbook / Ontario Home
Economics Association ; edited by Mairlyn Smith.

Includes index.

ISBN 978-1-77050-097-6

1. Cooking (Quinoa). 2. Vegetarian cooking.
3. Cookbooks.

I. Smith, Mairlyn II. Title.

TX393.O68   2012   641.6'31   C2011-908302-7

The publisher acknowledges the financial support of the
Government of Canada through the Canada Book Fund
(CBF) and the Province of British Columbia through the
Book Publishing Tax Credit.

13 14 15 16 5 4 3

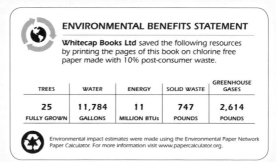

ENVIRONMENTAL BENEFITS STATEMENT

Whitecap Books Ltd saved the following resources
by printing the pages of this book on chlorine free
paper made with 10% post-consumer waste.

TREES	WATER	ENERGY	SOLID WASTE	GREENHOUSE GASES
25	11,784	11	747	2,614
FULLY GROWN	GALLONS	MILLION BTUs	POUNDS	POUNDS

Environmental impact estimates were made using the Environmental Paper Network
Paper Calculator. For more information visit www.papercalculator.org.

Contents

Foreword

THIS WONDERFUL COOKBOOK could not have been possible without the extremely talented and dedicated Mairlyn Smith, PHEc. When Mairlyn called me up with the idea of Ontario Home Economics Association members collaborating on a quinoa cookbook for vegetarians, I quickly got excited. What better way to showcase our skills and share our love of healthy eating than with a cookbook about this nutritious new ingredient?

Looking back, however, I think we both underestimated the job. Coordinating the submissions and testing the recipes was a massive effort. Every single recipe was personally reviewed and tested by Mairlyn. But we ended up with more than just a collection of recipes: throughout the book, we hear Mairlyn's unique voice, as she teaches readers about quinoa in her characteristically approachable and entertaining way.

The Ontario Home Economics Association is so grateful for all the many hours of hard work and enthusiasm that Mairlyn put into this book. Because of her efforts, we have achieved something we can all be proud of. Thanks Mairlyn, for a job well done and for being an amazing role model for all professional home economists.

Amy Snider-Whitson, PHEc
President, Ontario Home Economics Association,
March 2010–12

Slow Cooker Vegetarian
Lasagna (page 128)

Preface

The answer isn't easy because a brilliant idea can hit you at the weirdest times and in the oddest places; at a grocery store, in a yoga class, walking in the park or when your publisher gives you a call.

Case in point: I was away at my friend's cottage relaxing, when I decided to check my landline for messages (note to self: work on relaxing skills). Aside from messages from my mom, my son and a couple of friends, there was a message from Whitecap's CEO, Michael Burch. I immediately returned his call. Here's the mini version of the conversation:

"I have a great idea for a new cookbook that I'd love you to write."

"Great!" (Ego getting stroked.) "What's the idea?"

"A quinoa cookbook for vegetarians."

(My foodie brain kicks in and realizes this *is* a brilliant idea.)

"Brilliant idea!" (Note to self: try to be more creative in comebacks.)

And so the seed was planted and my brain went into overdrive. How could I make this cookbook different? What could I create that would make it stand out?

When I need to solve a problem I take my dog for a walk in my local park, and somewhere between the bridge and the forest I had one of those lightbulb moments—why not make this cookbook a collaboration of recipes written by my "peeps"—my fellow professional home economists. We could bring different experiences and foodie backgrounds to the subject as well as enlighten consumers as to who we were as a profession, all at the same time. Brilliant!

I called Amy Snider-Whitson, then acting president of the Ontario Home Economics Association (OHEA), and asked if we as an association could write the book together. Many board meetings later, plus conversations back and forth with OHEA members and the publisher, we had a result—this book, which I believe proves that professional home economists know a thing or two about healthy eating.

Thanks to all of my fellow professional home economists and students at various universities (see their bios at the back of the book) who answered the call and wrote the informative and delicious recipes contained in this book. These talented and dedicated people submitted recipes that reflect an eclectic palate. They range in age from their 20s to their 70s and bring a range of life experiences, from trainee home economists to retired home economists. Above all, they demonstrate the dedication and expertise of professional home economists everywhere.

Professional home economists work in all areas of the public and private sectors. We use our specialized education and training to assist people in enhancing their daily lives. A provincial act respecting the OHEA recognizes

Warm Quinoa with Beets
and Swiss Chard (page 93)

the right of individuals who have met the membership qualifications to use the designation Professional Home Economist (PHEc). As professionals we are committed to empowering individuals and families with the knowledge and skills to achieve and maintain a desirable quality of life. We are educated and knowledgeable in areas that affect Canadian families such as nutrition, food production and preparation, clothing and textiles, child development, housing, household finances, consumer issues and family relationships. Home economists work in fields that include education, journalism, recipe development, food styling, international development, consumer consulting and more. Visit ohea.on.ca to learn more about what it means to be a professional home economist, and how we can help Canadians live better lives.

On behalf of the 58 professional home economists and students who contributed to this cookbook, I wish you all peace, love and fibre.

Mairlyn Smith

Introduction

JUST BECAUSE QUINOA LOOKS LIKE A GRAIN, and some food manufacturers label quinoa a grain, and you can cook quinoa like a grain, doesn't mean it *is* a grain. This superfood is actually a *seed*.

Professional home economists love solving a good food mystery. So we went on a mission to find out why some packages say "whole grain" and others don't.

Is it a whole grain or a seed?

Unfortunately, after hours spent deciphering endless amounts of quinoa research, we are stumped. The best we can do is to give you our professional opinion. The naming or misnaming of this nutrient-dense little gem may have started in translation. Depending on what you read, you'll find that in Peru, where this seed originated, the Incas called quinoa either the "Mother of Grains" or the "Mother Seed."

According to the Whole Grains Council, quinoa (*Chenopodium quinoa*, or goosefoot) is a pseudo-cereal. This is the name the council gives to foods that are eaten and cooked like grains but are in fact not grains. Seed, grain and now pseudo-cereal? What's a person to think? Whatever *you* decide to call this potent little superstar, the most important thing is to recognize the coveted place quinoa holds in vegetarian cooking. This little bundle of goodness gets an A+ for protein quality.

Quinoa growing in Peru (photos on facing page and above: Barb Holland)

This potent little superstar holds a coveted place in vegetarian cooking and gets an A+ for protein quality.

Varieties of quinoa brands

Stats on a superfood

Nutrient information
per ½ cup (125 mL)
cooked quinoa

Calories	88 kcal
Fat	1 g
Protein	3 g
Carbohydrates	16 g
Fibre	2 g
Manganese	0.5 mg
Magnesium	47 mg
Iron	1 g
Phosphorus	111 mg
Folate	31 µg

Source: Canadian
Nutrient File, 2007

Why the hoopla about a seed?

Complete proteins contain all the essential amino acids that help the body build and repair itself. These are the type of proteins found in animal sources, like poultry, fish and red meat. Finding a complete protein in the plant world is a challenge, and this is quinoa's claim to fame. As a complete protein, quinoa provides your body with all those essential amino acids, making it a smart choice for vegans and vegetarians alike.

Soy is also a superstar in the plant protein department, but is a challenge to most North American cooks. Enter ancient quinoa. This mild-tasting, easy-to-cook little seed is a protein source that can be eaten and enjoyed by many. Aside from being a complete protein, one serving of quinoa is an excellent source of manganese, a good source of magnesium and phosphorus and a source of folate.

Manganese helps to maintain normal blood sugar levels, promotes the optimal function of your thyroid gland and helps to maintain the health of your nerves. Magnesium is needed in every organ of your body. It also helps relax blood vessels, which may in turn help reduce blood pressure. Phosphorus is needed for the growth, maintenance and repair of all tissues and cells. Folate, one of the amazing B vitamins, helps the nervous system function properly and aids in the production of DNA.

What kind should I buy?

Knowing that quinoa is a seed can still lead you on a wild quinoa hunt. Some commercial brands call quinoa a "whole grain" right on the package. Adding to the confusion, different brands of quinoa may require different amounts of cooking

time. Some packages state 8 to 10 minutes to cook, others 15 to 20 minutes. This got us wondering. Why would the same food item require different cooking times to produce the same end result? Had certain brands of quinoa been processed, thus requiring less cooking?

To answer this question, let's look at the makeup of quinoa a little more closely. The seed has a bitter resin called saponin. It can be removed at the manufacturing level by an alkaline water wash or by mechanical abrasion. The latter results in the seed becoming pearled or polished as it removes more than just the bitter resin, but also part of the pericap or germ. Removing this outer layer reduces the cooking time, but it also destroys some of the nutrients. All this means is that you have two ways to choose the quinoa that will give you the most nutrients:

- Read the required cooking time given on the package. The type of quinoa used in this book requires 15 to 20 minutes' cooking time. If a package states 8 to 10 minutes, the quinoa has been through some sort of mechanical processing.

- Look for the word "unpolished" on the label.

Variety is the spice of life

The Whole Foods Council states that there are over 120 different varieties of quinoa. However, only a few are grown commercially, and they

The lighter the colour, the milder the flavour.

| For small yields of cooked quinoa (¾ cup/185 mL to 1½ cups/375 mL), use a small, 1½ qt (1.5 L) saucepan. | For medium yields of cooked quinoa (1¾ cups/435 mL to 2½ cups/625 mL), use a medium, 2½ qt (2.5 L) saucepan. | For larger yields of cooked quinoa (3 cups/750 mL to 3½ cups/875 mL), use a large, 3½ qt (3.5 L) saucepan. |

come in the following shades: white (ranging from ivory to pale yellow), red and black. If you've cooked with only the white variety, try expanding your culinary horizons with red, black or mixed quinoa. Since quinoa is even now grown in Canada, choose local when possible and support Canadian farmers.

As quinoa cooks, the colourful coating (the technically correct term is the pericap or germ) around each tiny seed starts to curl off. The end result is a teeny-tiny-looking spiral. Depending on the variety, the cooked quinoa can taste extremely mild to slightly nutty. Colour is usually a good indicator of flavour—the lighter the colour, the milder the flavour. Choose the white variety for a mild flavour and red or black for a nuttier flavour. The darker the colour of the quinoa, the chewier the texture as well.

Where can I buy quinoa?
There was a time, and not even that long ago, when no one knew what quinoa was. With this food product's ever-growing popularity, most people now know what it is, can find it in a regular grocery store, can pronounce it correctly (KEEN-wah) and can even spell it. You can buy quinoa or any number of products made from quinoa in larger grocery stores, in health food stores, in bulk food stores and at Costco.

Choose local when possible and support Canadian farmers.

Storing quinoa
Even though quinoa isn't a grain, store it as you would a grain—in a tightly sealed container in a cool, dark, dry place. Quinoa does contain some fat and as a result it can go rancid. To extend its shelf life, store it in the fridge or freezer.

Cooking quinoa
Ever eaten bitter quinoa? We hope not; aside from tasting bitter the outer coating, called saponin, is a toxin. To get rid of the saponin, rinse quinoa really well before cooking. Don't be surprised to see a soapy lather or bubbles; this is the saponin being rinsed away. It's best to rinse every brand of quinoa, even the brands that say they are prewashed (erring on the side of caution).

You will need a heavy-bottomed saucepan with a tight-fitting lid. The size of the saucepan matters as well. See photos on this page. Overcrowding the saucepan will yield soggy cooked quinoa.

Through many taste tests, we found that the method described on the facing page produces the best cooked quinoa.

When cooking quinoa to use right away in a recipe such as a salad, to speed up cooling, spread the cooked quinoa on a clean, dry baking sheet and let sit until completely cooled.

How much does it make?
For hot cooked quinoa, the ratio of quinoa to water is usually 1:2. Said another way, use one portion of uncooked quinoa to two portions of liquid. Some recipes in the book are cooked differently, as the instructions reflect the best ratio for that specific recipe.

1. Measure the quinoa in a dry measuring cup. See the chart on page 6 for quantities.

2. Rinse the quinoa in a fine-mesh wire strainer under cold running water.

3. Measure the water or broth in a glass measuring cup.

4. Place the quinoa in a saucepan, add the water or broth and bring to a rolling boil.

5. Cover, reduce heat to medium-low and cook for 15 to 20 minutes.

6. The quinoa is cooked when the grains are translucent and all the liquid has been absorbed.

7–8. Fluff with a fork, remove from heat and let stand covered for 5 to 10 minutes. (The quinoa is shown uncovered in the Step 8 photo.)

Recipe uses cooked quinoa as an ingredient; see table at right for instructions and amounts if you need to cook quinoa from scratch

Recipe uses a bread machine

Recipe uses a microwave oven

Recipe uses a slow cooker

Gluten free

SAUCEPAN SIZE	QUINOA	WATER	COOKED QUINOA
Small 1½ qt (1.5 L)	¼ cup (60 mL)	+ ½ cup (125 mL)	= ¾ cup (185 mL)
	⅓ cup (80 mL)	+ ⅔ cup (160 mL)	= about 1 cup (250 mL)
	½ cup (125 mL)	+ 1 cup (250 mL)	= about 1½ cups (375 mL)
Medium 2½ qt (2.5 L)	¾ cup (185 mL)	+ 1½ cups (375 mL)	= about 2–2½ cups (500–625 mL)
Large 3½ qt (3.5 L)	1 cup (250 mL)	+ 2 cups (500 mL)	= 3–3½ cups (750–875 mL)
	1½ cups (375 mL)	+ 3 cups (750 mL)	= 4½–5 cups (1.125–1.25 L)

About the recipes

Make sure that you are within the range of sodium consumption set out by Health Canada. (The amount of sodium considered adequate to promote good health in adults is 1,500 mg per day but Health Canada recommends that adults do not exceed 2,300 mg of sodium per day (www.hc-sc.gc.ca).

We have added minimal to no salt to these recipes but for flavour we opted to use a regular vegetable broth whenever broth was called for. This decision still leaves a great majority of the recipes within the sodium guidelines. It's still important to check the label and choose a brand that contains no more than 500 mg sodium per 1 cup (250 mL) serving.

These recipes were designed to keep the sodium per serving in check. However, if you are concerned or have dietary restrictions, you may further reduce the sodium content by using reduced-salt vegetable broths. Adjust the quantity of other seasonings such as fresh herbs to boost the flavour.

Every one of the 120 recipes in this book uses some form of quinoa, from the seed version to quinoa flour, flakes or puffs.

To make the recipes more economical, to support local farmers and to provide improved flavour, recipes have been written seasonally. So near the top of each recipe, you will see particular seasons listed or an indication that a recipe is appropriate year round.

To help you navigate your way through the recipes, we have used various icons at the top of certain recipes (see sidebar) Looking for gluten free? 🌾 We have you covered. Does the recipe require cooked quinoa? The icon 🍲 will alert you to this before you start preparing the recipe.

Feel free to change the recipes and use red, black or mixed in any of the recipes that use regular quinoa. Different types of quinoa will give each dish a different flavour note. Don't worry about changing cooking times for the different colours of quinoa—cooking times are the same right across the board.

The nutrient breakdowns at the end of each recipe will help you see at a glance the number of calories and the amount of fat, sodium, carbohydrates, cholesterol, fibre, protein and sugars in each serving. We believe that knowledge is power and the more you know, the better able you are to make healthy decisions.

Calories matter, so to help you on your journey to good vegetarian health there isn't a main course recipe that is over 500 calories per serving.

Knowledge is power and the more you know, the better able you are to make healthy decisions.

From top: Quinoa puffs, quinoa flakes, quinoa flour

The many faces of quinoa

Nowadays you may buy quinoa in a variety of different forms. Aside from the colourful seeds, it is sold as puffs, flakes and flour. Quinoa is also added to or used in pasta, crackers, cereals, wraps and breakfast bars, with the list expanding yearly.

Quinoa flour

When baking, you can generally replace up to 20 percent of the wheat flour with quinoa flour in most recipes. Quinoa flour contains higher amounts of both protein and fat than regular flour. To extend its shelf life and prevent the flour from becoming rancid, store it in a cool, dry place in a sealed container. Store quinoa flour in your fridge for up to 3 months or freezer for up to 6 months.

Quinoa flakes and quinoa puffs

You can find quinoa flakes or puffs in the cereal section of larger grocery stores, at most health food stores and at some bulk food stores. The flakes have been rolled and flattened like rolled oats, and the puffs have been popped similar to puffed wheat. Both can be eaten for breakfast.

To cook quinoa flakes, combine equal amounts of flakes and boiling water, stir, bring back to a boil and cook uncovered for 1½ minutes, stirring constantly.

Serve with toppings you would add to cooked porridge or oatmeal (for example, fresh or dried fruit, yogurt). As for the quinoa puffs, just add milk and eat as you would any regular cold breakfast cereal. We have used both the flakes and the puffs in recipes in the book (see Quinoameal Raisin Cookies on page 149 and Fruit and Nut Clusters on page 179).

More and more varieties of quinoa pasta products are becoming available. Most are a combination of rice flour and quinoa flour and can be found in larger grocery stores, most health food stores and some bulk food stores.

Tips on gluten free

If you are living a gluten free lifestyle, the more you know about being gluten free the better. With so much misinformation about foods and products that contain gluten, your best bet is to go to the authority in the field, the Canadian Celiac Association (see Online Resources, page 188). The association provides information and a gluten-free diet plan. It also has several comprehensive lists of the foods that people living with celiac disease need to avoid, need to question and can have in their diets.

Quinoa is gluten free and, as a result, many of the recipes in this cookbook are gluten free. Gluten-free recipes have this icon ⊚. Many of the other recipes in the book can be made gluten free if you use gluten-free versions of the following ingredients:

- baking powder
- soy sauce
- rolled oats (the label must specify "pure, non-contaminated gluten-free oats")
- bouillion or broth cubes or stock
- sour cream
- quinoa pasta shells.

The following products may contain gluten and their labels must be carefully checked:

- rice paper sheets
- Asian or Thai chili sauce
- pesto sauce.

Whole spices are gluten free but it is always a good idea to check the labels of the following:

- garam masala
- seasoning or spice blends
- curry powder
- pumpkin pie spice.

Vegetable preparation tips

Professional home economists love to share cooking and food shopping tips and tricks. Here are some that apply to the recipes in this book.

1. **CLEANING AND CHOPPING LEEKS:** Cut off the top and the root. Make a cut from top to bottom but not through the leek. Run under cold water to remove dirt. Slice into coins.

2. **CUTTING JULIENNE:** Using a sharp knife, slice peppers, carrots or other vegetables as thinly as possible. Go for matchstick size or slightly bigger.

3. **MAKING A CHIFFONADE:** Roll the leaves of leafy greens (kale and mint are shown in the photo), then slice into very thin strips.

Deseeding a pomegranate

There are many different ways to deseed a pomegranate.
This is the method we like.

1. Using a sharp paring knife, cut around the top core of
   the pomegranate.

2. Pull off the top core.

3. Score quarters on the peel.

4. For easier cleanup, place a bowl in the sink and, working
   over the bowl, remove the peel.

5. Pull or pop off the seeds. Remove as much of the bitter
   white membrane as possible.

6. And *voilà*!

Using wet parchment paper

Lining casserole pans with wet parchment paper prevents food from sticking to the pan, making cleanup easier at dishwashing time.

1. Hold a piece of parchment paper (about 6 inches/15 cm bigger than the pan you wish to line) under cold running water.

2–3. Scrunch up the paper under the water and then wring it out.

4. Shake off the excess water.

5. Line the pan.

6. The next time you make a dish like Cajun Stuffed Bell Pepper with Tomatoes (page 88), the cleanup will be so easy, you'll thank us.

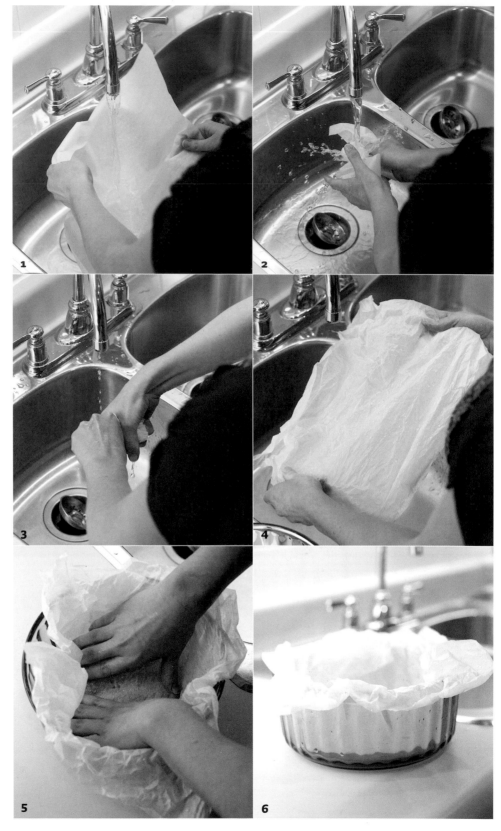

Breakfasts

Breakfasts

BREAKFAST HAS LONG BEEN TOUTED as the most important meal of the day and for good reason—unless you wake up your brain with a nutritious breakfast, you and your body aren't going to have the fuel you need to help you start your day. Making time to eat breakfast can be challenging, so here are some tips to help you pull off that all-important first meal of the day.

- If your breakfast is hot cereal (see recipes in this chapter), make it the night before and warm it up in the morning. Add more liquid—milk, soy beverage or juice (whatever the recipe called for)—and reheat.

- Serve all cereals with foods rich in vitamin C like oranges, grapefruit or berries to help your body absorb the iron in the cereal.

- Include a protein source like nuts to boost your protein for the day and help you feel fuller longer.

- If you don't have enough time for a sit-down breakfast, grab a serving of **Power Granola** (page 15), a yogurt and an orange to eat when you get to work.

- For a vegetarian, getting enough iron in your diet is a bit trickier than for non-vegetarians. Drinking tea or coffee with breakfast will lower your body's ability to absorb non-heme iron (found in vegetarian sources). Best to wait and have that cuppa tea or mugga java at least two hours after you've eaten.

Start your day off right with this warm porridge plus antioxidant-rich dried blueberries and apricots and, rounding out the whole shebang—heart-healthy walnuts.

YEAR ROUND

Heather Howe, PHEc

Creamy Fruit and Nut Porridge   ½ Oatmeal — try or Rice

1. Place the quinoa in a large saucepan, add the soy beverage or milk and salt (if using), and bring to a gentle boil. Reduce heat to low, cover and gently simmer for 20 to 25 minutes, stirring occasionally to prevent sticking.

2. Remove from heat and stir in the dried blueberries, dried apricots and cinnamon. Cover and let stand for 10 minutes, until the fruit is plumped up and the quinoa has absorbed most of the liquid. (The porridge will be creamy.)

3. **TO SERVE:** Sprinkle each serving with 1 Tbsp (15 mL) of nuts and a drizzle of maple syrup or to taste.

Makes 4 cups (1 L) • One serving = ½ cup (125 mL) (without optional salt)

1 cup (250 mL)	quinoa, rinsed and drained
3 cups (750 mL)	organic soy beverage — Almond Milk or skim milk Oatmeal
Pinch	salt (optional)
⅓ cup (80 mL)	dried blueberries
⅓ cup (80 mL)	slivered dried apricots
½ tsp (2 mL)	cinnamon
½ cup (125 mL)	chopped walnuts
2 Tbsp (30 mL)	pure maple syrup

Any leftovers can be stored covered in the fridge for up to 3 days. Reheat either on top of the stove or in the microwave, adding more soy beverage or milk. Sprinkle with nuts and drizzle with maple syrup at serving time.

Nutrition per serving

217 calories	8 g total fat	1 g saturated fat
0 mg cholesterol	43 mg sodium	32 g carbohydrates
2 g fibre	12 g sugars	6 g protein

Excellent source of vitamin D, calcium, magnesium, iron and zinc.

January in Canada means dark and stormy nights, but on a positive note it also means that citrus from the United States is in season. This citrusy spin on a bowl of hot quinoa is a great way to wake up your taste buds during the winter doldrums. The added bonus of vitamin C from the cranberries will help your body absorb the iron from the quinoa.

Citrus and Cranberry Hot Cereal

1 cup (250 mL)	quinoa, rinsed and drained
1 cup (250 mL)	home-style orange juice
1 cup (250 mL)	water
½ cup (125 mL)	dried cranberries or cherries
Zest of 1	orange
1	orange, peel removed, fruit cut into bite-sized pieces
½ cup (125 mL)	chopped walnuts

1. Place the quinoa in a medium saucepan, add the orange juice and water and bring to a boil. Reduce heat to low and simmer covered for 15 to 20 minutes. The quinoa is done when the grains are translucent and most of the liquid has been absorbed.

2. Fluff with a fork and remove from heat. Fold in the dried cranberries, orange zest and orange segments. Cover and let stand for 5 to 10 minutes.

3. **TO SERVE:** Sprinkle each serving with 1 Tbsp (15 mL) of walnuts.

Makes 4 cups (1 L) • One serving = ½ cup (125 mL)

Nutrition per serving

175 calories	6 g total fat	1 g saturated fat
0 mg cholesterol	7 mg sodium	27 g carbohydrates
3 g fibre	10 g sugars	4 g protein

This granola is flavourful and crunchy. It can be added as a topping to yogurt or sprinkled on top of either plain cooked quinoa flakes or your favourite hot cereal. Remember, size really does matter when it comes to health and calories—a serving of this granola is only ¼ cup (60 mL).

YEAR ROUND

Erin MacGregor, PHEc

Power Granola

1. Preheat the oven to 250°F (120°C). Line a large baking sheet (11- × 17-inch/28 × 42 cm) with parchment paper.

2. In a large bowl, combine the quinoa, oats, almonds, coconut, flaxseed and sesame seeds.

3. In a separate medium bowl, whisk together the oil, maple syrup, brown sugar, cinnamon and water. Pour this over the quinoa mixture and stir until combined. Spread evenly over the baking sheet.

4. Bake for 1 hour, stirring every 15 minutes, until the granola is evenly toasted.

5. **TO SERVE:** Add the cranberries. Enjoy as a breakfast cereal, sprinkle on top of yogurt or eat as a snack. Store in an airtight container for up to 1 month.

Makes 3 cups (750 mL) • One serving = ¼ cup (60 mL)

¼ cup (60 mL)	quinoa, soaked for 8 hours or overnight in water then well rinsed and drained
1 cup (250 mL)	large-flake rolled oats
½ cup (125 mL)	whole almonds, coarsely chopped
¼ cup (60 mL)	unsweetened shredded coconut
2 Tbsp (30 mL)	ground flaxseed
2 Tbsp (30 mL)	sesame seeds
2 Tbsp (30 mL)	canola oil
2 Tbsp (30 mL)	pure maple syrup
2 Tbsp (30 mL)	brown sugar, packed
½ tsp (2 mL)	cinnamon
2 tsp (10 mL)	water
½ cup (125 mL)	dried cranberries

Nutrition per serving

163 calories	8 g total fat	1 g saturated fat
0 mg cholesterol	12 mg sodium	20 g carbohydrates
3 g fibre	8 g sugars	4 g protein

These light and fluffy gluten-free pancakes are great for a weekend breakfast. Leftover pure pumpkin purée can be frozen for the next time you make these, or use it immediately in the Pumpkin Oatmeal Chocolate Chip Muffins on page 24.

Pumpkin Cornmeal Pancakes

1¾ cups (435 mL)	buttermilk (see sidebar page 22)
½ cup (125 mL)	pure pumpkin purée
1 Tbsp (15 mL)	brown sugar, packed
1	omega-3 egg
1½ Tbsp (22 mL)	canola oil, divided
1 cup (250 mL)	brown rice flour
½ cup (125 mL)	quinoa flour (see page 7)
½ cup (125 mL)	whole-grain medium-grind cornmeal (see sidebar)
1 Tbsp (15 mL)	pumpkin pie spice
1 tsp (5 mL)	cinnamon
1 tsp (5 mL)	baking soda
	Pure maple syrup for serving

Not all cornmeal is whole-grain cornmeal. Look for "Whole Grain" on the package and choose medium-grind for this recipe. Find it in the health food section of larger grocery stores. The brand we used was Bob's Red Mill.

1. In a large bowl, whisk together the buttermilk, pumpkin purée, brown sugar, egg and 1 Tbsp (15 mL) of the oil.

2. Whisk in the brown rice and quinoa flours, cornmeal, pumpkin pie spice, cinnamon and baking soda until well combined. Heat a large non-stick frying pan over medium heat. Lightly coat with the remaining 1½ tsp (7 mL) canola oil.

3. Stir batter once more (it will be thick). If batter is too thick, add an extra ¼ cup (60 mL) buttermilk or water. Spoon 2 Tbsp (30 mL) of the batter into the pan. Use the back of the tablespoon to spread out the batter to make a 4-inch (10 cm) pancake. Pancake will be ready to flip when the underside is golden brown and there are bubbles on the top.

4. Flip and cook the pancake until the centre springs back when pressed. If desired, keep all of the pancakes in an oven set at 200°F (95°C) until all the batter is cooked.

5. **TO SERVE:** Drizzle pancakes with a little pure maple syrup—nothing says *Canada* quite like real maple syrup.

Makes 20 four-inch (10 cm) pancakes • **One serving = 4 pancakes (without syrup)**

Nutrition per serving (without syrup)

322 calories	7 g total fat	1 g saturated fat
43 mg cholesterol	229 mg sodium	56 g carbohydrates
4 g fibre	8 g sugars	10 g protein

Pumpkin Cornmeal Pancakes

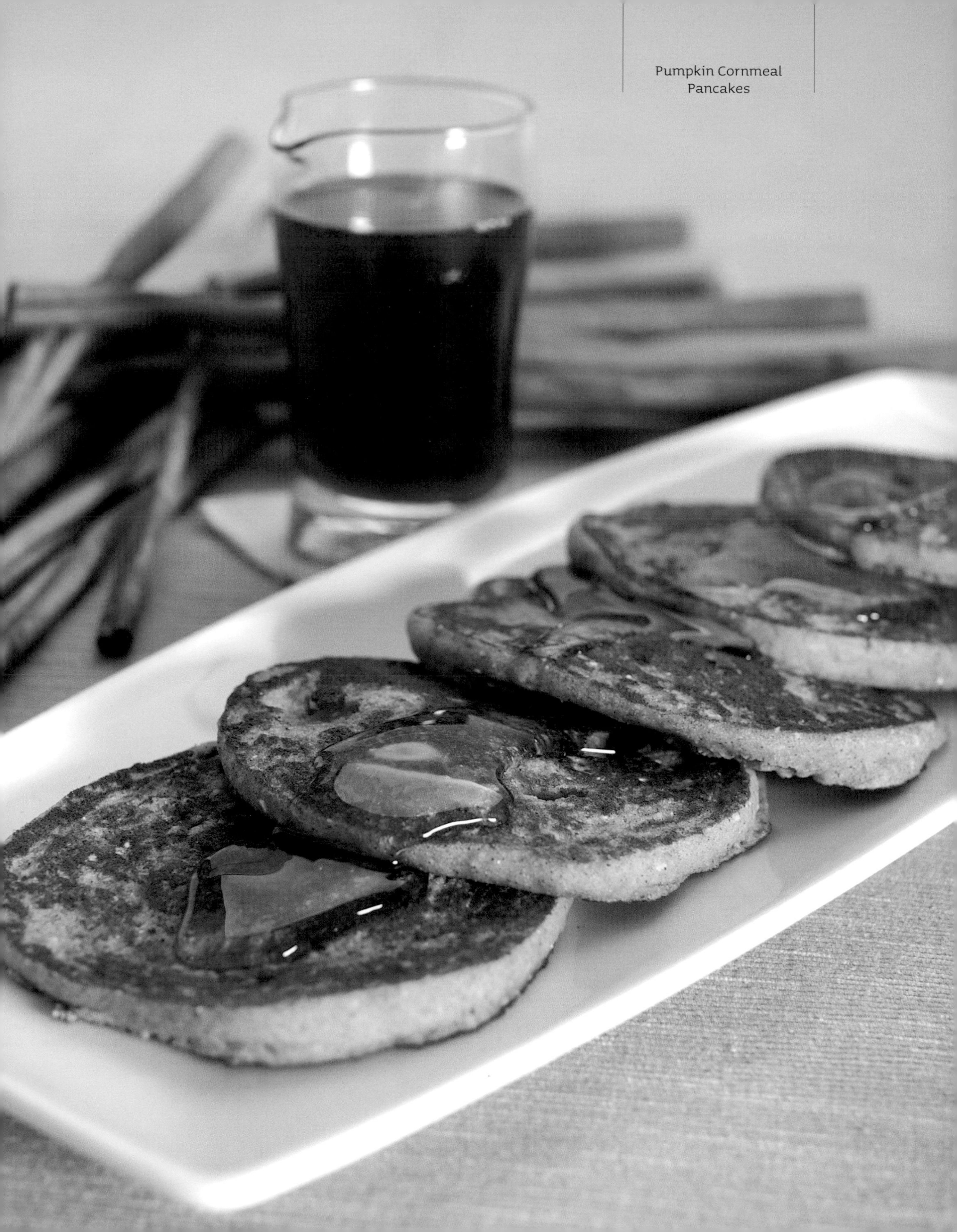

Quickbreads and Yeast Breads

CHAPTER TWO

Quickbreads and Yeast Breads

IF YOU WERE ONE OF THE LUCKY PEOPLE who took Grade 8 Home Economics, then you probably remember the Muffin Method. All the Home Ec teachers who contributed to this book certainly hope so. Once mastered, this useful method can be used to whip up a batch of muffins or a yummy loaf. For those of you who may have missed it (or need a refresher), here's how it goes:

1. Mix all the dry ingredients in one bowl.

2. Mix all the wet (liquid) ingredients in a second bowl.

3. Add the wet ingredients to the dry ingredients and stir just until combined.

4. Spoon into the prepared pan and bake.

The main difference between muffins and loaves, quickbread and yeast bread is the leavener. All quickbreads get their leavening power from either baking powder or baking soda or both. Breads made with yeast get their leavening powers from—wait for it—yeast. (Some answers are just too simple.)

Muffins can be either sweet or savoury (both kinds feature in this chapter). They have become a big part of our Canadian fast-food cuisine. Unfortunately, most commercially prepared muffins are loaded with fat and sugar—empty calories—and can be a barren wasteland in terms of fibre. The muffin and loaf recipes in this chapter break that mould. All of the muffins and one serving of the loaf recipes contain 2 to 5 grams of fibre, and all contain less than 220 calories per serving. Now off you go to try some of these creations. Hope you get an A.

NOTE: Because quinoa flour does not contain any gluten, baked goods made with it, including the recipes here, tend to be denser than products that use gluten-rich all-purpose or whole wheat flour.

Looking to boast your calcium and magnesium intake? The dried figs are the answer in this nutrient-dense muffin.

Fig Bran Muffins

1. Preheat the oven to 375°F (190°C). Line a 12-cup muffin pan with non-stick paper liners.

2. In a medium bowl, combine the figs and milk. Let stand while preparing recipe and preheating oven.

3. In a large bowl, whisk together the whole wheat and quinoa flours, bran, wheat germ, baking powder, baking soda and salt.

4. Add the egg to the fig mixture and beat with a fork to blend. Add the brown sugar, molasses, oil and vanilla, blending well.

5. Stir the liquid mixture into the dry mixture just until blended. Using an ice cream scoop, spoon the batter into each prepared muffin cup.

6. Bake in the centre of the oven for 16 to 18 minutes, or until a toothpick inserted in the centre of a muffin comes out clean.

7. Set the pan to cool on a wire rack for 5 minutes. Remove muffins from pan and let them cool completely on the wire rack. Store in an airtight container for up to 2 days, or freeze for up to 2 months.

Makes 12 muffins • One serving = 1 muffin

1 cup (250 mL)	chopped, dried figs (about 4 oz/125 g), preferably Black Mission
1 cup (250 mL)	1% milk
1 cup (250 mL)	whole wheat flour
¼ cup (60 mL)	quinoa flour (see page 7)
¾ cup (185 mL)	natural wheat bran
1 Tbsp (15 mL)	wheat germ, untoasted
2 tsp (10 mL)	baking powder
½ tsp (2 mL)	baking soda
Pinch	salt
1	omega-3 egg
⅓ cup (80 mL)	dark brown sugar, packed
⅓ cup (80 mL)	molasses
¼ cup (60 mL)	canola oil
1 tsp (5 mL)	pure vanilla extract

Nutrition per serving

188 calories	6 g total fat	1 g saturated fat
17 mg cholesterol	126 mg sodium	33 g carbohydrates
4 g fibre	18 g sugars	4 g protein

Excellent source of magnesium.

FALL and **WINTER**

Janet Buis, PHEc

Fresh local apples and protein-rich quinoa make this low-fat, high-fibre, whole-grain muffin a favourite for breakfast, school lunches or an afternoon snack. It's ideal when smeared with a bit of honey or apple butter.

Apple Bran Muffins

½ cup (125 mL)	quinoa flour (see page 7)
½ cup (125 mL)	whole wheat flour
2 Tbsp (30 mL)	wheat germ
1½ tsp (7 mL)	baking powder
½ tsp (2 mL)	baking soda
1 Tbsp (15 mL)	cinnamon
½ cup (125 mL)	raisins
½ cup (125 mL)	diced apple, scrubbed well, peel left on
½ cup (125 mL)	brown sugar, packed
2 Tbsp (30 mL)	canola oil
¼ cup (60 mL)	applesauce, unsweetened
¼ cup (60 mL)	fancy molasses
2	omega-3 eggs
1 cup (250 mL)	buttermilk (see sidebar)
½ tsp (2 mL)	pure vanilla extract
1½ cups (375 mL)	wheat bran
2 Tbsp (30 mL)	oat bran

No buttermilk in the fridge? Substitute 1 cup (250 mL) 1% milk plus 1 Tbsp (15 mL) vinegar whisked together for these muffins. Vary quantities as needed for other recipes.

1. Preheat the oven to 425°F (220°C). Line a 12-cup muffin pan with paper liners.

2. In a medium bowl, whisk together the quinoa and whole wheat flours, wheat germ, baking powder, baking soda and cinnamon. Stir in the raisins and apple.

3. In a large bowl, whisk together the brown sugar, oil and applesauce until smooth. Beat in the molasses and eggs. Stir in the buttermilk, vanilla and wheat and oat brans.

4. Carefully fold the flour mixture into the apple sauce/molasses mixture, stirring just until blended. Do not overmix. Using an ice cream scoop, spoon ⅓ cup (80 mL) of the batter into each prepared muffin cup.

5. Bake in the centre of the oven for 18 to 20 minutes, or until a toothpick inserted in the centre of a muffin comes out clean.

6. Set the pan to cool on a wire rack for 5 minutes. Remove muffins from pan and let them cool completely on the wire rack. Store in an airtight container for up to 2 days, or freeze for up to 2 months.

Makes 12 large muffins • One serving = 1 muffin

Nutrition per serving

184 calories	4 g total fat	1 g saturated fat
33 mg cholesterol	87 mg sodium	35 g carbohydrates
5 g fibre	19 g sugars	5 g protein

Excellent source of magnesium.

These moist and flavourful muffins, made with quinoa flakes and a punch of ginger, are sure to please the rhubarb aficionados in the crowd.

SPRING and SUMMER

Jennifer MacKenzie, PHEc

Rhubarb Muffins

1. Preheat the oven to 375°F (190°C). Line a 12-cup muffin pan with paper liners or spray with canola oil.

2. Set 1 Tbsp (15 mL) of the quinoa flakes aside. In a large bowl, whisk together the remaining quinoa flakes, flour, wheat germ, baking powder, baking soda and salt (if using).

3. In a separate medium bowl, whisk together the egg, yogurt, honey, oil, ginger and cinnamon until blended.

4. Pour the wet ingredients over the dry ingredients and sprinkle with the rhubarb. Stir just until moistened. Using an ice cream scoop, spoon the batter into each prepared muffin cup. Sprinkle with the reserved quinoa flakes.

5. Bake in the centre of the oven for about 25 minutes, or until a toothpick inserted in the centre of a muffin comes out clean. Muffin tops should be golden and spring back when lightly touched.

6. Set the pan to cool on a wire rack for 5 minutes. Remove muffins from pan and let them cool completely on the wire rack. Store in an airtight container for up to 2 days, or freeze for up to 2 months.

Makes 12 muffins • One serving = 1 muffin

1 cup (250 mL)	quinoa flakes, divided (see page 7)
1¼ cups (310 mL)	whole wheat flour
2 Tbsp (30 mL)	wheat germ
2 tsp (10 mL)	baking powder
½ tsp (2 mL)	baking soda
¼ tsp (1 mL)	salt (optional)
1	omega-3 egg
1 cup (250 mL)	1% plain yogurt
½ cup (125 mL)	liquid honey
¼ cup (60 mL)	canola oil
1 Tbsp (15 mL)	minced fresh ginger (or 1 tsp/5 mL ground ginger)
¼ tsp (1 mL)	cinnamon
1½ cups (375 mL)	chopped fresh or frozen rhubarb, thawed slightly

Nutrition per serving

178 calories	6 g total fat	1 g saturated fat
17 mg cholesterol	105 mg sodium	28 g carbohydrates
2 g fibre	14 g sugars	5 g protein

Pumpkin is rich in beta carotene, an antioxidant that may help reduce your chances of developing certain cancers. This recipe is a great way to get it into your diet more often.

Pumpkin Oatmeal Chocolate Chip Muffins

½ cup (125 mL)	quinoa flour (see page 7)
½ cup (125 mL)	whole wheat flour
1 cup (250 mL)	large-flake rolled oats
1 tsp (5 mL)	baking powder
½ tsp (2 mL)	baking soda
1 Tbsp (15 mL)	cinnamon
1¼ cups (310 mL)	pure pumpkin purée
½ cup (125 mL)	brown sugar, packed
1	omega-3 egg
1 Tbsp (15 mL)	canola oil
¼ cup (60 mL)	dark chocolate chips, at least 60% cocoa mass

1. Preheat the oven to 375°F (190°C). Line a 12-cup muffin pan with non-stick paper liners or spray with canola oil.

2. In a medium bowl, whisk together the quinoa and whole wheat flours, oats, baking powder, baking soda and cinnamon, blending well.

3. In a large bowl, whisk together the pumpkin purée, brown sugar, egg and oil.

4. Carefully fold the flour mixture into the pumpkin mixture just until blended. Add the chocolate chips and gently combine all ingredients. Using an ice cream scoop, spoon the batter into each prepared muffin cup.

5. Bake in the centre of the oven for 18 to 20 minutes, or until a toothpick inserted in the centre of a muffin comes out clean.

6. Set the pan to cool on a wire rack for 5 minutes. Remove muffins from pan and let them cool completely on the wire rack. Store in an airtight container in the fridge for up to 1 week, or freeze for up to 1 month.

Makes 12 muffins • One serving = 1 muffin

Nutrition per serving

159 calories	4 g total fat	1 g saturated fat
16 mg cholesterol	70 mg sodium	27 g carbohydrates
3 g fibre	12 g sugars	4 g protein

Oranges and dates are a perfect complement for each other in these muffins. Look for soft pitted dates in the produce section rather than the firm pressed dates in the baking aisle.

Orange Date Muffins

1. Preheat the oven to 375°F (190°C). Line a 12-cup muffin pan with non-stick paper liners.

2. In a large bowl, whisk together the whole wheat and quinoa flours, brown sugar, wheat germ, baking powder and baking soda.

3. In a blender, process the orange pieces, dates, buttermilk, oil and egg until the oranges and dates are well chopped but not mushy (you want some texture).

4. Stir the orange mixture into the dry mixture just until blended. Using an ice cream scoop, spoon the batter into each prepared muffin cup.

5. Bake in the centre of the oven for 16 to 18 minutes, or until a toothpick inserted in the centre of a muffin comes out clean.

6. Set the pan to cool on a wire rack for 5 minutes. Remove muffins from pan and let them cool completely on the wire rack. Store in an airtight container for up to 2 days, or freeze for up to 2 months.

Makes 12 muffins · One serving = 1 muffin

1¼ cups (310 mL)	whole wheat flour
¼ cup (60 mL)	quinoa flour (see page 7)
3 Tbsp (45 mL)	brown sugar, packed
1 Tbsp (15 mL)	wheat germ
1½ tsp (7 mL)	baking powder
½ tsp (2 mL)	baking soda
1	orange, with peel, cut into pieces and seeds removed
1 cup (250 mL) (about 5 oz/150 g)	pitted dates
¾ cup (185 mL)	buttermilk (see sidebar page 22)
¼ cup (60 mL)	canola oil
1	omega-3 egg

Baking dates, compressed into cakes, can be found in the baking aisle of the supermarket. Loose dates are usually found in the produce aisle.

Nutrition per serving

167 calories	6 g total fat	1 g saturated fat
17 mg cholesterol	49 mg sodium	27 g carbohydrates
4 g fibre	12 g sugars	4 g protein

These muffins are brimming with the antioxidant power of blueberries. Use fresh local berries in season or frozen local berries out of season.

Blueberry Muffins

½ cup (125 mL)	quinoa, rinsed and drained
¾ cup (185 mL)	1% milk
1 cup (250 mL)	whole wheat flour
1½ tsp (7 mL)	baking powder
½ tsp (2 mL)	baking soda
½ tsp (2 mL)	ground cardamom
⅓ cup (80 mL)	non-hydrogenated margarine
½ cup (125 mL)	brown sugar, packed
1	omega-3 egg
1 tsp (5 mL)	grated lemon rind
2 Tbsp (30 mL)	fresh lemon juice
1 cup (250 mL)	fresh or frozen blueberries

1. Preheat the oven to 400°F (200°C). Line 9 muffin cups in a 12-cup pan with paper liners or spray with canola oil.

2. In a small saucepan, combine the quinoa with the milk. Bring to a boil over medium-high heat. Reduce heat to low, cover and cook for 15 minutes. Remove from heat and let stand for 5 minutes, or until all the liquid has been absorbed.

3. In a medium bowl, whisk together the flour, baking powder, baking soda and cardamom.

4. In a large bowl, using a wire whisk or handheld mixer, beat together the non-hydrogenated margarine and brown sugar until fluffy. Beat in the egg, lemon rind and juice until combined. Stir in the quinoa mixture. Add the flour mixture and stir just until moistened. Gently fold in the blueberries.

5. Divide the batter among the 9 muffin cups. Add about 1 Tbsp (15 mL) of water to each empty muffin cup to prevent the pan from warping.

6. Bake in the centre of the oven for 20 to 25 minutes, or until a toothpick inserted in the centre of a muffin comes out clean.

7. Set the pan to cool on a wire rack for 5 minutes. Remove muffins from pan and let them cool completely on the wire rack. Store in an airtight container for up to 2 days, or freeze for up to 2 months.

Makes 9 muffins • One serving = 1 muffin

Nutrition per serving

218 calories	9 g total fat	2 g saturated fat
22 mg cholesterol	192 mg sodium	32 g carbohydrates
3 g fibre	15 g sugars	5 g protein

Serve these savoury muffins with one of the three different bowls of chili on pages 114–116 for a weekend family dinner. Add a tossed green salad and you're all set in the health department.

FALL and **WINTER**

Mary Carver, PHEc

Savoury Cornmeal Muffins

1. Preheat the oven to 400°F (200°C). Line a 12-cup muffin pan with non-stick paper liners or spray with canola oil.

2. In a large bowl, whisk together the whole wheat and quinoa flours, cornmeal, baking powder, baking soda and pepper.

3. In a medium bowl, whisk together the eggs, buttermilk and oil. Stir in the green onions, cheese and red pepper.

4. Add the wet ingredients to dry ingredients and mix just until combined. Using an ice cream scoop, spoon the batter into each prepared muffin cup (cups will be very full).

5. Bake in the centre of the oven for 20 to 24 minutes, or until a toothpick inserted in the centre of a muffin comes out clean.

6. Set the pan to cool on a wire rack for 5 minutes. Remove muffins from pan and let them cool completely on the wire rack. Store in an airtight container for up to 2 days, or freeze for up to 2 months.

Makes 12 muffins • One serving = 1 muffin

2 cups (500 mL)	whole wheat flour
½ cup (125 mL)	quinoa flour (see page 7)
½ cup (125 mL)	whole-grain medium-grind cornmeal (see sidebar page 16)
2 tsp (10 mL)	baking powder
½ tsp (2 mL)	baking soda
½ tsp (2 mL)	freshly ground black pepper
2	omega-3 eggs
1⅓ cups (330 mL)	buttermilk (see sidebar page 22)
¼ cup (60 mL)	canola oil
1 cup (250 mL)	thinly sliced green onions (about 1 bunch)
½ cup (125 mL)	grated Parmesan Reggiano cheese
¼ cup (60 mL)	finely diced red pepper

Nutrition per serving

194 calories	8 g total fat	2 g saturated fat
37 mg cholesterol	175 mg sodium	24 g carbohydrates
4 g fibre	2 g sugars	8 g protein

Your kitchen will smell like a winter holiday every time you bake this loaf. It's perfect for brunches or great as a snack. Calorie wise, one slice is one serving.

YEAR ROUND

Michele McAdoo, PHEc

Orange and Date Holiday Bread

1. Preheat the oven to 375°F (190°C). Lightly grease a 9- × 5-inch (2 L) loaf pan with canola oil or line with parchment paper.

2. In a large bowl, whisk together all three flours, the sugar, baking soda and baking powder.

3. In a blender, process the orange pieces and juice until the orange peel is finely chopped.

4. Add the dates, eggs and margarine. Blend just until combined (a few short whirls).

5. Add the orange mixture to the flour mixture and stir just until moistened. Spoon the batter into the prepared loaf pan and level off the top.

6. Bake in the centre of the oven for 45 to 50 minutes, or until a toothpick or cake tester inserted in the centre comes out clean. Set the pan to cool on a wire rack for 10 minutes. Remove loaf from pan and let it cool completely on the rack before slicing. Store in an airtight container for up to 3 days, or freeze for up to 3 months.

Makes 1 loaf (16 slices) · One serving = 1 slice

½ cup (125 mL)	whole wheat flour
¼ cup (60 mL)	all-purpose flour
¾ cup (185 mL)	quinoa flour (see page 7)
¾ cup (185 mL)	granulated sugar
1 tsp (5 mL)	baking soda
1 tsp (5 mL)	baking powder
1 large	orange, with peel, cut into pieces and seeds removed
½ cup (125 mL)	orange juice
½ cup (125 mL)	chopped pitted dates (see page 25)
2	omega-3 eggs
½ cup (125 mL)	non-hydrogenated margarine

Nutrition per serving

165 calories	7 g total fat	1 g saturated fat
24 mg cholesterol	79 mg sodium	24 g carbohydrates
2 g fibre	13 g sugars	2 g protein

Excellent source of vitamin D.

SUMMER and
EARLY FALL

Anna Shier,
OHEA student member

No time for a sit-down breakfast? Make this delicious, not-too-sweet breakfast quickbread for those mornings when you're on the go. Freeze individual slices. The night before, pack one into your purse, briefcase or lunch bag so as you dash out the door, it'll be thawed and ready to eat when you are.

Zucchini and Pecan Bread

¾ cup (185 mL)	whole wheat flour
¼ cup (60 mL)	quinoa flour (see page 7)
¼ cup (60 mL)	ground flaxseed
1 tsp (5 mL)	baking soda
1 tsp (5 mL)	baking powder
1 Tbsp (15 mL)	cinnamon
1 tsp (5 mL)	ground nutmeg
1	omega-3 egg
¼ cup (60 mL)	buttermilk (see sidebar page 22)
½ cup (125 mL)	applesauce, unsweetened
1 tsp (5 mL)	pure vanilla extract
½ cup (125 mL)	brown sugar, packed
1 cup (250 mL)	zucchini, peel on, coarsely grated
¾ cup (185 mL)	cooked quinoa made with water (see pages 5–6)
½ cup (125 mL)	chopped pecans

1. Preheat the oven to 350°F (175°C). Lightly grease a 9- × 5-inch (2 L) loaf pan with canola oil or line with parchment paper.

2. In a large bowl, whisk together the whole wheat and quinoa flours, flaxseed, baking soda, baking powder, cinnamon and nutmeg.

3. In a medium bowl, whisk together the egg, buttermilk, applesauce, vanilla and brown sugar until blended. Fold in the grated zucchini, cooked quinoa and chopped pecans until well blended.

4. Pour the zucchini mixture into the flour mixture and stir until well combined. Pour the batter into the prepared loaf pan.

5. Bake in the centre of the oven for 45 to 50 minutes, or until a toothpick or cake tester inserted in the centre comes out clean.

6. Set the pan to cool on a wire rack for 5 minutes. Remove loaf from pan and let it cool completely on the rack. Store in an airtight container for up to 3 days, or freeze for up to 3 months.

Makes 1 loaf (12 slices) · One serving = 1 slice

Nutrition per serving

146 calories	5 g total fat	1 g saturated fat
16 mg cholesterol	107 mg sodium	22 g carbohydrates
3 g fibre	11 g sugars	4 g protein

Excellent source of vitamin D.

Magnesium has been shown to help reduce the chances of stroke. This light and delicious bread just so happens to be an excellent source of this important mineral. Also a source of protein, this higher-fibre loaf also freezes well. (See photo page 32.)

YEAR ROUND

Joan Ttooulias, PHEc

Red Quinoa and Pumpkin Seed Bread

1. Line two 9- × 5-inch (2 L) loaf pans with parchment paper. Set aside.

2. In a large bowl, measure 9 cups (2.25 L) of the flour. Add the wheat germ, pumpkin seeds, salt and yeast. Slowly pour in the warm water and the cooked quinoa. On a flat surface, mix together and knead the dough for 10 minutes. Use only as much of the remaining flour until you have achieved a soft, elastic, very slightly sticky dough.

3. Return to bowl, cover with plastic wrap and let rise for 2 hours, or until doubled in size.

4. Punch down the dough and let rise for another hour, covered in the bowl. Punch down the dough again, divide it in half and shape into two loaves. Place dough into the prepared loaf pans and let rise for final proof, 45 to 60 minutes. Meanwhile, preheat the oven to 425°F (220°C).

5. Bake loaves for 10 minutes, then reduce oven heat to 400°F (200°C) and bake for another 25 to 30 minutes, or until a cake tester inserted in the centre of a loaf comes out clean.

6. Remove from pans and let the loaves cool completely on a wire rack before slicing. Wrap well and freeze for up to one month.

Makes 2 loaves (16 slices each) • One serving = 1 slice

9 to 10 cups (2.25 to 2.5 L)	whole wheat flour
½ cup (125 mL)	wheat germ
½ cup (125 mL)	unsalted pumpkin seeds
1½ Tbsp (22 mL)	kosher salt (see sidebar page 33)
1 Tbsp (15 mL)	quick-rise yeast
4 cups (1 L)	warm water
3 cups (750 mL)	cooked red quinoa made with water (see pages 5–6)

Nutrition per serving

154 calories	2 g total fat	0 g saturated fat
0 mg cholesterol	325 mg sodium	30 g carbohydrates
5 g fibre	1 g sugars	6 g protein

Excellent source of magnesium.

Gluten-Free Ancient Grains Bread (foreground), Red Quinoa and Pumpkin Seed Bread (background) (page 31)

This bread uses three types of non-traditional flour (sorghum, amaranth and quinoa) plus cornmeal for good measure. You can find all of these types of flours in larger health food stores.

YEAR ROUND

Donna Washburn, PHEc,
& Heather Butt, PHEc

Gluten-Free Ancient Grains Bread
(Mixer Method)

1. Lightly grease a 9- × 5-inch (2 L) loaf pan with canola oil.

2. In a large bowl, combine the sorghum and amaranth flours, cornmeal, quinoa flour, tapioca starch, brown sugar, xanthan gum, yeast and salt. Mix well and set aside.

3. In a separate bowl, using a heavy-duty electric mixer with paddle attachment, combine the eggs, egg white, water, canola oil and vinegar until well blended. With the mixer on its lowest speed, slowly add the dry ingredients until combined. Stop the machine and scrape the bottom and sides of the bowl with a spatula. With the mixer on medium speed, beat for 4 minutes.

4. Pour the batter into the prepared loaf pan. Let rise, uncovered, in a warm, draft-free place for 60 to 75 minutes, or until dough has risen to the top of the pan. Meanwhile, preheat the oven to 350°F (175°C).

5. Bake in the centre of the oven for 35 to 45 minutes, or until loaf sounds hollow when tapped on the bottom. Remove from pan immediately and let loaf cool completely on a wire rack before slicing.

Makes 1 loaf · One serving = 1 slice

1 cup (250 mL)	sorghum flour
⅔ cup (160 mL)	amaranth flour
½ cup (125 mL)	cornmeal
¼ cup (60 mL)	quinoa flour (see page 7)
⅓ cup (80 mL)	tapioca starch
⅓ cup (80 mL)	brown sugar, packed
1 Tbsp (15 mL)	xanthan gum (see sidebar page 35)
1 Tbsp (15 mL)	bread machine or instant yeast
1½ tsp (7 mL)	salt (don't omit— see sidebar)
2	omega-3 eggs
1	omega-3 egg white (see sidebar)
1 cup (250 mL)	water
2 Tbsp (30 mL)	canola oil
1 tsp (5 mL)	apple cider vinegar

Never omit salt from a yeast bread recipe. It has an important function in yeast development.

When using only an egg white in a recipe, save the yolk and make an omelette the same day for dinner. Add the extra yolk for extra nutrients.

Nutrition per serving

128 calories	3 g total fat	0 g saturated fat
25 mg cholesterol	267 mg sodium	22 g carbohydrates
3 g fibre	5 g sugars	3 g protein

YEAR ROUND

Donna Washburn, PHEc,
& Heather Butt, PHEc

Similar to Gluten-Free Ancient Grains Bread (Mixer Method) on page 33, this recipe uses a bread machine instead. It combines a quartet of healthy grains—sorghum, amaranth, cornmeal and quinoa—in a soft-textured, nutritious loaf that's perfect for sandwiches.

Gluten-Free Ancient Grains Bread
(Bread Machine Method)

1 cup (250 mL)	sorghum flour
¾ cup (185 mL)	amaranth flour
¾ cup (185 mL)	cornmeal
¼ cup (60 mL)	quinoa flour (see page 7)
½ cup (125 mL)	tapioca starch
⅓ cup (80 mL)	packed brown sugar
1 Tbsp (15 mL)	xanthan gum (see sidebar)
¾ tsp (4 mL)	bread machine or instant yeast
1½ tsp (7 mL)	salt (see sidebar page 33)
1¼ cups (310 mL)	water
2 Tbsp (30 mL)	canola oil
1 tsp (5 mL)	cider vinegar
2	omega-3 eggs, lightly beaten
2	omega-3 egg whites, lightly beaten (see sidebar page 33)

1. In a large bowl, combine the sorghum and amaranth flours, cornmeal, quinoa flour, tapioca starch, brown sugar, xanthan gum, yeast and salt. Mix well and set aside.

2. Pour the water, oil and vinegar into the bread machine baking pan. Add the eggs and egg whites.

3. Select the Dough Cycle. As the bread machine is mixing, gradually add the dry ingredients, scraping the bottom and sides of pan with a spatula. Try to incorporate all the dry ingredients within 1 to 2 minutes. When the mixing and kneading are complete, remove the kneading blade, leaving the bread pan in the bread machine. Quickly smooth the top of the loaf. Allow the cycle to finish. Turn off the bread machine.

4. Select the Bake Cycle. Set the timer to 60 minutes and the temperature to 350°F (175°C). Allow the cycle to finish. Do not turn off the machine before taking the internal temperature of the loaf with an instant-read thermometer. It should be 200°F (95°C). If it's between 180°F (82°C) and 200°F (95°C), leave machine on the Keep Warm Cycle until baked. If it's below 180°F (82°C), turn on the Bake Cycle and check the internal temperature every 10 minutes. (Some bread machines are automatically set for 60 minutes; others need to be set by 10-minute intervals.)

5. Once the loaf has reached 200°F (95°C), remove from pan immediately and let cool completely on a wire rack before slicing.

CONTINUED ON NEXT PAGE

GLUTEN-FREE CYCLE ADJUSTMENTS

If your bread machine has a Gluten-Free Cycle, make the following adjustments:

1. Warm the water to between 110°F and 115°F (43°C and 46°C).

2. Warm the eggs and egg whites.

3. Follow the recipe instructions, but select the Gluten-Free Cycle rather than the Dough Cycle and Bake Cycle.

4. At the end of the Gluten-Free Cycle, take the temperature of the loaf using an instant-read thermometer. It should be 200°F (95°C). If it's between 180°F (82°C) and 200°F (95°C), leave machine on the Keep Warm Cycle until baked. If it's below 180°F (82°C), turn on the Bake Cycle and check the internal temperature every 10 minutes. (Some bread machines are automatically set for 60 minutes; others need to be set by 10-minute intervals.)

Makes 1 loaf • One serving = 1 slice

Xanthan gum is a natural carbohydrate produced from the fermentation of glucose. It helps prevent baked goods from crumbling, gives them greater volume, improves their texture and extends their shelf life. It also helps to prevent pastry fillings from weeping, so your crust won't get soggy. *Do not omit it from the recipe.* NOTE: Xanthan gum can be purchased from health food stores, online or where you purchase other gluten-free ingredients. Before working with xanthan gum, be sure to wipe counters and containers with a dry cloth; when it comes in contact with water, it becomes slippery, slimy and almost impossible to wipe up.

Nutrition per serving

134 calories	3 g total fat	0 g saturated fat
25 mg cholesterol	273 mg sodium	23 g carbohydrates
2 g fibre	5 g sugars	3 g protein

Here's a quintet of healthy grains to go along with wheat—kamut, spelt, quinoa, flaxseed and millet seeds.

Historic Grains Bread

1½ cups (375 mL)	water
⅓ cup (80 mL)	skim milk powder
1¼ tsp (6 mL)	salt (see sidebar page 33)
3 Tbsp (45 mL)	liquid honey
3 Tbsp (45 mL)	canola oil
2½ cups (625 mL)	all-purpose flour or bread flour
⅓ cup (80 mL)	kamut flour
⅓ cup (80 mL)	quinoa flour (see page 7)
⅓ cup (80 mL)	spelt flour
⅓ cup (80 mL)	flaxseed, cracked or lightly ground
3 Tbsp (45 mL)	millet seed
1¼ tsp (6 mL)	bread machine yeast

1. Measure ingredients into bread machine baking pan in order recommended by the manufacturer.

2. Insert baking pan into oven chamber. Select Basic or White Cycle, 2 lb size and a medium crust setting.

3. When the machine finishes baking, turn off the machine and with oven mitts carefully remove the bread pan. Remove the loaf from the bread pan and allow to cool completely on a rack before slicing.

Makes 1 loaf • One serving = 1 slice

Nutrition per serving

89 calories	4 g total fat	0 g saturated fat
0 mg cholesterol	267 mg sodium	22 g carbohydrates
3 g fibre	5 g sugars	3 g protein

CHAPTER THREE

Soups

Soups

PUT DOWN THE CAN OPENER and walk away from that ready-to-serve commercial soup. Instead, mosey on over to the fridge and pantry to find a cache of ingredients that will help you create a big pot of love. Homemade soups, so versatile and so easy to make, can start a meal or be the meal itself, served with crackers (try those on page 49) or a salad.

No matter what the ingredients, soups give you a sense of comfort and can keep you warm on a cold night. They make your whole home smell wonderful, and can contain a bowl chock-full of nutrients. Next time the winds are howling and the rain or snow is falling, a steaming pot of soup can be the answer to "What's for dinner tonight?"

This sunset orange–hued soup is mildly spiced, making it family friendly. If you like a bit more heat, increase the cayenne pepper. Quinoa has a double function in this recipe—not only does it add some protein to a vegetable soup, but it helps to thicken the soup as well. NOTE: For even more fibre, leave the peel on the sweet potatoes. Just scrub them well and chop.

FALL and WINTER

Barb Holland, PHEc

Sweet Potato and Tomato Soup

1. In a large soup pot or Dutch oven, heat the oil over medium heat. Add the onions and sweet potatoes and sauté about 4 to 6 minutes, until slightly softened.

2. Add the garlic, ginger and spices to the vegetables and sauté for another minute.

3. Add the quinoa, tomatoes and broth. Bring to a boil. Reduce heat to low, cover and simmer about 20 minutes, until the sweet potatoes are tender.

4. Using an immersion or free-standing blender, purée the soup as smooth or as chunky as you like. Return to the pot. Add the chickpeas and heat through, about 3 minutes.

5. **TO SERVE:** Remove from heat and stir in the spinach until the leaves are just wilted. Store in the fridge for up to 3 days.

Makes 10 cups (2.5 L) • One serving = 2 cups (500 mL)

1 Tbsp (15 mL)	canola oil
1	onion, chopped
1 large (about 1 lb/500 g)	sweet potato, peeled and chopped
3	cloves garlic, minced
1 Tbsp (15 mL)	minced or grated fresh ginger
1 tsp (5 mL)	ground coriander
1 tsp (5 mL)	ground cumin
1 tsp (5 mL)	paprika
¼ tsp (1 mL)	freshly ground black pepper
¼ tsp (1 mL)	cayenne pepper
½ cup (125 mL)	quinoa, rinsed and drained
1 can (28 oz/796 mL)	diced tomatoes, no salt added
4 cups (1 L)	vegetable broth
1 can (19 oz/540 mL)	chickpeas, well rinsed and drained
2 cups (500 mL)	well-packed baby spinach leaves, stems removed

Nutrition per serving

318 calories	5 g total fat	0 g saturated fat
0 mg cholesterol	459 mg sodium	61 g carbohydrates
10 g fibre	13 g sugars	11 g protein

Excellent source of vitamin A and iron.

A bowl of lemony flavours plus the protein from both the egg and the quinoa make this a great lunch or first course at dinner. It's low in calories but high in flavour, which means you can have seconds without second thoughts.

Egg, Lemon and Arugula Soup

6 cups (1.5 L)	vegetable broth
3 cloves	garlic, minced
¼ tsp (1 mL)	red pepper flakes
⅓ cup (80 mL)	quinoa, rinsed and drained
2	omega-3 eggs
¼ cup (60 mL)	fresh lemon juice
3 Tbsp (45 mL)	finely grated Parmesan cheese
2 cups (500 mL)	well-packed arugula, chiffonade (see page 8)
½ tsp (2 mL)	freshly ground black pepper
	Finely chopped green onions or parsley for garnish

1. In a large soup pot or Dutch oven over medium-high heat, combine the vegetable broth, garlic and red pepper flakes. Bring to a boil and add the quinoa. Reduce heat to medium-low; partially cover and simmer for 20 minutes.

2. Meanwhile, in a medium bowl, whisk together the eggs with the lemon juice and Parmesan cheese until fluffy. Whisking constantly, gradually stir the egg mixture into the hot broth mixture.

3. Stir in the arugula and remove from heat. Season with pepper to taste.

4. **TO SERVE:** Ladle the soup into deep bowls and sprinkle with green onions or parsley. Store in the fridge for up to 3 days.

Makes 6 cups (1.5 L) • One serving = 1 cup (250 mL)

Arugula is a dark leafy green with a peppery flavour that goes really well with the lemon in this recipe. For a milder version of the soup, use baby spinach.

Nutrition per serving

108 calories	4 g total fat	1 g saturated fat
68 mg cholesterol	534 mg sodium	14 g carbohydrates
2 g fibre	3 g sugars	6 g protein

Excellent source of vitamin A.

Kale is a nutrient powerhouse of folate, that amazing B vitamin that can help protect your DNA. Health Canada recommends that you eat at least one serving of dark leafy greens a day, and kale is one of those leafy greens they're talking about.

FALL and **WINTER**

Astrid Muschalla, PHEc

Hearty Kale Soup

1. In a large soup pot or Dutch oven, heat the oil over medium. Add the onion, garlic, carrots and celery and sauté about 5 to 10 minutes, until slightly softened.

2. Stir in the garam masala, cayenne pepper and bay leaves. Rub the thyme and oregano leaves between your palms to help release more of the flavours. Add them to the pot and sauté another minute.

3. Add the water, tomatoes, lentils and quinoa. Bring to a boil, then reduce heat to low and simmer uncovered for about 20 minutes.

4. **TO SERVE:** Stir in the kale and cook for another 2 minutes. Remove the bay leaves and season with balsamic vinegar. Serve immediately. Store in the fridge for up to 3 days, or freeze for up to 2 months.

Makes 8 cups (2 L) • One serving = 1 cup (250 mL)

1 Tbsp (15 mL)	canola oil
1	onion, diced
3	cloves garlic, minced
2	medium carrots, scrubbed well and sliced into ½-inch (1 cm) coins
1	celery stalk, diced
1–2 tsp (5–10 mL)	garam masala (see sidebar)
¼ tsp (1 mL)	cayenne pepper
2	bay leaves
1 tsp (5 mL)	dried thyme leaves
1 tsp (5 mL)	dried oregano leaves
5 cups (1.25 L)	water
1 can (28 oz/796 mL)	diced tomatoes
1 cup (250 mL)	dry brown lentils, well rinsed and drained
½ cup (125 mL)	quinoa, rinsed and drained
2 cups (500 mL)	fresh kale, chiffonade (see page 8)
2 Tbsp (30 mL)	balsamic vinegar

Garam masala is a blend of 10 to 12 spices used in Northern Indian cooking. Sweeter than and not as hot as some Indian spice blends, it adds a fabulous flavour to this soup.

Nutrition per serving

119 calories	3 g total fat	0 g saturated fat
0 mg cholesterol	374 mg sodium	21 g carbohydrates
5 g fibre	6 g sugars	4 g protein

This is a great way to add more dairy and calcium to your family's diet. This golden-coloured, mild-tasting soup is a bowl of comfort food for a cold winter night. Don't let the addition of the oatmeal scare you off; it's used as a thickener and provides some heart-healthy soluble fibre as well.

Leek Comfort Soup

2 Tbsp (30 mL)	extra virgin olive oil
3	cloves garlic, minced
1 tsp (5 mL)	ground cumin
1 tsp (5 mL)	ground coriander
1 tsp (5 mL)	turmeric
½ cup (125 mL)	quinoa, rinsed and drained
¼ cup (60 mL)	large-flake rolled oats
2	medium carrots, scrubbed well and coarsely chopped
1	red pepper, coarsely chopped
4 cups (1 L)	vegetable broth
2	medium leeks, cleaned, trimmed, white part only, sliced into thin coins (see page 8)
1 can (19 oz/540 mL)	chickpeas, well rinsed and drained
2 cups (500 mL)	skim milk or organic soy beverage

1. In a large soup pot or Dutch oven, heat the oil over medium heat. Add the garlic and sauté for 1 minute. Add the spices and sauté for 2 to 3 minutes. You will smell the amazing aromas.

2. Add the quinoa, rolled oats, carrots, red pepper and broth. Bring to a boil, then reduce heat to low and simmer covered for 6 minutes.

3. Add the sliced leeks and chickpeas. Return soup to a boil, then reduce heat to low and simmer covered for another 15 minutes.

4. When the leeks are soft, stir in the milk or soy beverage and let simmer for 2 minutes.

5. **TO SERVE:** Ladle the soup into bowls and serve immediately. Store in the fridge for up to 2 days.

Makes 8 cups (2 L) • One serving = 1⅓ cups (330 mL)

Nutrition per serving

266 calories	8 g total fat	1 g saturated fat
2 mg cholesterol	526 mg sodium	40 g carbohydrates
6 g fibre	11 g sugars	11 g protein

Excellent source of vitamin A, vitamin C and iron.

This quick dinner is so easy to make that every university student should have it in their repertoire. NOTE: To add more protein, add 1 cup (250 mL) cubed tofu in Step 3.

YEAR ROUND

Linda Lichtenberger,
PHEc

Quick Egg-Drop Soup

1. In a medium saucepan over medium heat, bring the broth to a boil.

2. Add the quinoa and mushrooms. Return soup to a boil, then reduce heat to low and simmer covered for 15 minutes, or until the mushrooms and quinoa are both cooked.

3. Add the peas and green onions. Return soup to a boil, then reduce heat and stir to create a whirlpool. Keep stirring in the same direction as you slowly pour in the eggs in a thin stream. The egg will cook in less than a minute in the hot soup in long streams. Swirl and serve.

Makes 5 cups (1.25 L) • One serving = 1 cup (250 mL)

4 cups (1 L)	vegetable broth
¼ cup (60 mL)	quinoa, rinsed and drained
8 oz (235 g)	white or cremini mushrooms, thinly sliced (about 3 cups/750 mL)
1½ cups (375 mL)	frozen green peas, no need to thaw
3	green onions, thinly sliced
2	omega-3 eggs, lightly beaten

Nutrition per serving

114 calories	3 g total fat	1 g saturated fat
76 mg cholesterol	504 mg sodium	15 g carbohydrates
3 g fibre	5 g sugars	7 g protein

FALL and WINTER

Carolyn Frail, PHEc

This recipe provides a great way to get several servings of vegetables (carrot, tomatoes, spinach) in one bowl of mildly spicy soup. Your body is going to love you for this one.

Zesty Minestrone

2 Tbsp (30 mL)	extra virgin olive oil
1	onion, coarsely chopped
1	large carrot, scrubbed well and coarsely chopped
1 cup (250 mL)	chopped celery
3	cloves garlic, minced
1 tsp (5 mL)	curry powder
¼ tsp (1 mL)	ground nutmeg
5 cups (1.25 L)	vegetable broth
1 cup (250 mL)	water
1 can (28 oz/796 mL)	diced tomatoes, no salt added
½ cup (125 mL)	quinoa, rinsed and drained
1 can (19 oz/540 mL)	kidney beans, well rinsed and drained
3 cups (750 mL)	baby spinach leaves

1. In a large soup pot or Dutch oven, heat the oil over medium heat. Add the onion and sauté for 3 to 5 minutes, or until soft.

2. Add the carrots, celery and garlic. Sauté until the vegetables are golden, about 5 minutes. Add the curry powder and nutmeg and sauté for another minute.

3. Add the broth, water, tomatoes, quinoa and beans. Bring to a boil, then reduce heat to low. Cover and simmer for 15 to 20 minutes, or until the quinoa is tender.

4. **TO SERVE:** Remove from heat and stir in the spinach until the leaves are just wilted. Serve with store-bought crackers or make your own (see recipe page 49). Store in the fridge for up to 3 days.

Makes 13 cups (3.25 L) • One serving = 1½ cups (375 mL)

Nutrition per serving

164 calories	5 g total fat	1 g saturated fat
0 mg cholesterol	358 mg sodium	26 g carbohydrates
6 g fibre	7 g sugars	7 g protein

Excellent source of vitamin A.

This hearty bowl of soul-warming, immunity-enhancing soup uses a mixture of both fresh and dried mushrooms to develop its fabulous earthy flavours. To make this soup as *wild* as you can, try using chanterelles, wood ears, shiitake and porcini. You can find dried mushrooms in most grocery stores in the produce section. NOTE: You will need a food processor for Step 1 to ensure optimum flavour.

Wild Mushroom Soup

1 Tbsp (15 mL)	extra virgin olive oil
2	medium leeks, cleaned, trimmed and sliced into thin coins (see page 8)
½ lb (250 g)	fresh mixed mushrooms, coarsely chopped
1	large sweet onion, coarsely chopped
2 tsp (10 mL)	Italian seasoning
1 tsp (5 mL)	freshly ground black pepper
½ oz (15 g)	dried mixed mushrooms
½ cup (125 mL)	quinoa, rinsed and drained
6 cups (1.5 L)	vegetable broth
2 cups (500 mL)	well-packed baby spinach

1. In a large soup pot or Dutch oven, heat the oil over low heat. Add the leeks, fresh mushrooms, onion, Italian seasoning and pepper. Cover and cook until the leeks are softened, about 15 minutes. Transfer mixture to a food processor and process until puréed.

2. Return mixture to the same pot. Add the dried mushrooms, quinoa and broth. Bring to a boil, then reduce heat to medium-low and cook covered for 25 to 30 minutes, or until the quinoa is very tender.

3. **TO SERVE:** Stir in the spinach and cook for 3 to 4 minutes, or until wilted. Serve immediately. Store in the fridge for up to 3 days.

Makes 12 cups (3 L) • One serving = 1½ cups (375 mL)

Nutrition per serving

119 calories	3 g total fat	0 g saturated fat
0 mg cholesterol	371 mg sodium	20 g carbohydrates
3 g fibre	5 g sugars	4 g protein

This robust, flavourful soup is more like a stew. If there are any leftovers, it tastes even better the next day.

FALL and WINTER

Amy Snider-Whitson, PHEc

African Peanut Soup with Red Quinoa

1. In a large soup pot or Dutch oven, heat the oil over medium heat. Add the shallots and cook, stirring often, for 5 minutes, or until golden brown. Add the garlic, curry powder, ginger and red pepper flakes. Stir while cooking for another 2 minutes.

2. Stir in the sweet potatoes until they are coated in spices. Stir in the broth, tomatoes, quinoa and peanut butter. Bring to a boil. Reduce heat to medium-low. Cover partially and simmer, stirring occasionally, for 20 minutes, or until the potatoes and quinoa are tender.

3. Add the lime juice. Season with pepper to taste. To purée or not to purée? For the best texture, purée half of the soup so there is a mixture of both smooth and chunky.

4. **TO SERVE:** Ladle the soup into deep bowls and garnish with cilantro and peanuts (if using). Store in the fridge for up to 3 days. Do not freeze.

Makes 9 cups (2.25 L) • One serving = 1½ cups (375 mL)

1 Tbsp (15 mL)	canola oil
3	shallots, chopped
2	cloves garlic, minced
1 Tbsp (15 mL)	curry powder
1 Tbsp (15 mL)	minced fresh ginger
¼ tsp (1 mL)	red pepper flakes
3 cups (750 mL)	peeled and diced sweet potatoes (about 2 medium)
4 cups (1 L)	vegetable broth
1 can (28 oz/796 mL)	diced tomatoes, no salt added
⅓ cup (80 mL)	red quinoa, rinsed and drained
½ cup (125 mL)	crunchy natural peanut butter (see sidebar)
	Juice of 1 small lime
2 tsp (10 mL)	freshly ground pepper, or to taste
¼ cup (60 mL)	finely chopped fresh cilantro for garnish
¼ cup (60 mL)	unsalted roasted peanuts for garnish (optional)

Widely available in grocery stores, natural peanut butter has no added sugar or fats and is *the* best choice for this recipe.

Nutrition per serving

294 calories	15 g total fat	2 g saturated fat
0 mg cholesterol	416 mg sodium	34 g carbohydrates
6 g fibre	11 g sugars	10 g protein

Excellent source of vitamin A.

The blend of herbs and spices in this invigorating soup will warm you up on cold days. Don't be surprised if this ends up becoming a family favourite. Make sure you use smoked paprika— it adds a fabulous flavour note. You can find smoked paprika in larger grocery stores.

Smoked Paprika and Lentil Soup

2 tsp (10 mL)	smoked paprika
1 tsp (5 mL)	red pepper flakes
½ tsp (2 mL)	ground allspice
1 Tbsp (15 mL)	canola oil
1	large baking potato (about 1½ cups/375 mL), peeled and chopped into about 1-inch (2.5 cm) chunks
2	medium carrots, scrubbed well and diced
1	large onion, chopped
2	large cloves garlic, finely chopped
¾ cup (185 mL)	dried lentils, well rinsed and drained
½ cup (125 mL)	quinoa, rinsed and drained
8 cups (2 L)	vegetable broth
1 can (28 oz/796 mL)	diced tomatoes
1	bay leaf
2	sprigs fresh rosemary
8 cups (2 L)	kale, stems removed, chopped into bite-sized pieces

1. In a small bowl, mix together the smoked paprika, red pepper flakes and allspice. Set aside.

2. In a soup pot or Dutch oven, heat the oil over medium-high heat. Add the potatoes, carrots, onion and garlic. Add the spice blend. Cook 7 to 8 minutes, until the vegetables have softened, stirring often to prevent sticking. If the mixture does stick, make sure to scrape up any bits. This adds flavour and will prevent the soup from burning.

3. Stir in the lentils, quinoa, broth, tomatoes, bay leaf and rosemary. Cover and bring to a boil. Reduce heat to medium-low and simmer for 15 minutes.

4. Add the chopped kale and cook for an additional 15 minutes, or until the lentils and quinoa are tender.

5. **TO SERVE:** Discard the bay leaf and rosemary sprigs before serving. Store in the fridge for up to 3 days.

Makes 13 cups (3.25 L) • One serving = 1½ cups (375 mL)

To reduce the sodium, use diced tomatoes that have no salt added.

Nutrition per serving

192 calories	5 g total fat	0 g saturated fat
0 mg cholesterol	667 mg sodium	33 g carbohydrates
7 g fibre	9 g sugars	7 g protein

Excellent source of vitamins A and C.

What's a bowl of soup without a cracker? Lonely. Make these crisp crackers to enjoy with dips or spreads and to serve with salads, or just top them with your favourite cheese. NOTE: You will need a coffee or spice grinder for this recipe and some upper body strength!

YEAR ROUND

Emily Richards, PHEc

Soup Crackers

1. Preheat the oven to 350°F (175°C). Line a large baking sheet (11- × 17-inch/28 × 42 cm) with parchment paper.

2. In a large non-stick frying pan over medium heat, toast the quinoa, stirring frequently, for about 10 to 15 minutes, or until it is fragrant and begins to snap, crackle and pop. NOTE: You really want the quinoa to be a deep golden brown, so just because you heard one quinoa seed snap or pop doesn't mean it's *all* ready. Patience...

3. Set aside the deep golden–brown quinoa in the frying pan and let cool slightly.

4. In small batches, place the quinoa in a coffee or spice grinder and grind until fine. Place in a bowl and set aside.

5. When all the quinoa has been ground, add the egg whites, butter, basil, oregano, rosemary and pepper. Stir until well combined.

6. Here's where you need some strength—using a large damp spatula, press the mixture firmly onto the prepared baking sheet, making sure you press it right to the edges. Alternatively, place a second piece of parchment paper on top of the mixture and use a rolling pin to roll out the dough right on the baking sheet. NOTE: The dough needs to be all the same thickness for the crackers to be crisp.

2 cups (500 mL)	quinoa, rinsed and well drained
1¼ cups (310 mL)	pasteurized egg whites (see sidebar)
¼ cup (60 mL)	butter, melted
¼ tsp (1 mL)	dried basil
¼ tsp (1 mL)	dried oregano leaves
¼ tsp (1 mL)	dried rosemary leaves
¼ tsp (1 mL)	freshly ground black pepper
½ tsp (2 mL)	sea salt or flaked salt like Maldon

You can find pasteurized egg whites where you find the regular eggs at the grocery store. Measure them using a glass measuring cup.

CONTINUED ON NEXT PAGE

7. Using a pizza cutter or paring knife, score the dough into about 2-inch (5 cm) squares. Sprinkle with sea salt. For a more rustic look like the one seen in the picture, bake whole and then break the sheet into pieces after it is completely cooled.

8. Bake in the centre of the oven for about 35 minutes, or until golden brown. Set the pan to cool completely on a wire rack. Carefully break the crackers along the scored lines. Store in an airtight container for up to 1 week.

Makes 48 crackers • **One serving = 3 crackers**

Nutrition per serving

114 calories	3 g total fat	3 g saturated fat
9 mg cholesterol	105 mg sodium	15 g carbohydrates
3 g fibre	0 g sugars	6 g protein

Excellent source of vitamin C.

CHAPTER FOUR

Salads

CHAPTER FOUR

Salads

Side Salads

Main Salads

TAKE ONE LARGE HANDFUL OF BABY GREENS, add a splash of oil and a sprinkle of vinegar, and ta-dah!—you have a simple salad. Even the ancient Romans and Greeks ate greens in a bowl with oil and vinegar. Too bad they thought the world was flat, or they could have taken a ship to Peru and enjoyed a hearty salad made with quinoa.

Served hot or cold, as a side or a main, these quinoa-inspired salads are made with nutrient-dense ingredients and all taste too good to be good for you.

Salads in which quinoa is paired with beans, lentils, tofu or nuts are higher in protein and work especially well as a main course. You can always have more than one serving to increase your protein intake (just keep an eye on calorie and sodium counts).

Combining guacamole with quinoa and adding romaine lettuce creates a distinctive salad. Make sure those heart-healthy avocadoes are ripe before you even think about making this. For a flavour twist add ½ cup (125 mL) of fresh cilantro.

Michele McAdoo, PHEc

Guacamole Salad

1. In a large bowl, gently toss together the lettuce, tomatoes, avocadoes and onions.

2. **DRESSING:** In a small bowl, whisk together the oil, lime juice, pepper, garlic and cayenne pepper (if using).

3. To serve, pour the dressing over the salad and toss gently to coat all the ingredients. Add the cooked quinoa and toss until evenly combined. Serve immediately.

Makes 12 cups (3 L) • One serving = 2 cups (500 mL)

10 cups (2.5 L)	torn romaine lettuce
2 cups (500 mL)	grape tomatoes, halved
2	ripe avocadoes, peeled, pitted and chopped
½ cup (125 mL)	thinly sliced red onions
3 cups (750 mL)	cooked quinoa made with vegetable broth (see pages 5–6)

DRESSING

2 Tbsp (30 mL)	extra virgin olive oil
¼ cup (60 mL)	freshly squeezed lime juice (about 2 limes)
½ tsp (2 mL)	freshly ground black pepper
1	clove garlic, minced
⅛ tsp (0.5 mL)	cayenne pepper (optional)

Nutrition per serving

298 calories	17 g total fat	2 g saturated fat
0 mg cholesterol	176 mg sodium	34 g carbohydrates
10 g fibre	5 g sugars	7 g protein

Excellent source of vitamin A, vitamin C, folate, magnesium and iron.

This colourful salad combines the flavours of lemon, shallots and parsley with the nutty, chewy texture of the wheat berries, making it a real winner. BONUS: It can be served either warm or cold.

Red Quinoa and Wheat Berry Salad

½ cup (125 mL)	wheat berries, well rinsed and drained (see sidebar)
2 cups (500 mL)	cooked red quinoa made with water (see pages 5–6)
½ cup (125 mL)	dried cranberries
⅓ cup (80 mL)	whole almonds, chopped
⅓ cup (80 mL)	chopped fresh parsley

DRESSING

Zest of 1	lemon
¼ cup (60 mL)	fresh lemon juice
2 Tbsp (30 mL)	minced shallot (about 1 shallot)
¼ cup (60 mL)	extra virgin olive oil
2 tsp (10 mL)	liquid honey
½ tsp (2 mL)	Dijon mustard

Wheat berries are the whole wheat kernel. Found in most health food or bulk food stores, they have a nutty flavour and offer a chewy texture to any dish.

1. In a medium saucepan, bring 1¼ cups (310 mL) of water to a boil. Stir in the wheat berries and return to a boil. Reduce heat to low, cover and simmer for 45 to 50 minutes, or until the wheat berries are tender. Remove from heat, drain any excess water and allow to cool slightly.

2. In a large bowl, toss together the cooked quinoa, wheat berries, cranberries, almonds and parsley.

3. **DRESSING:** In a medium bowl, whisk together the lemon zest and juice, shallots, oil, honey and Dijon mustard.

4. **TO SERVE:** Pour the dressing over the quinoa mixture and toss well. Serve immediately or store in the fridge for up to 3 days.

Makes about 4 cups (1 L) • One serving = ½ cup (125 mL)

opt: Barley

Nutrition per serving

296 calories	12 g total fat	1 g saturated fat
0 mg cholesterol	13 mg sodium	43 g carbohydrates
5 g fibre	9 g sugars	7 g protein

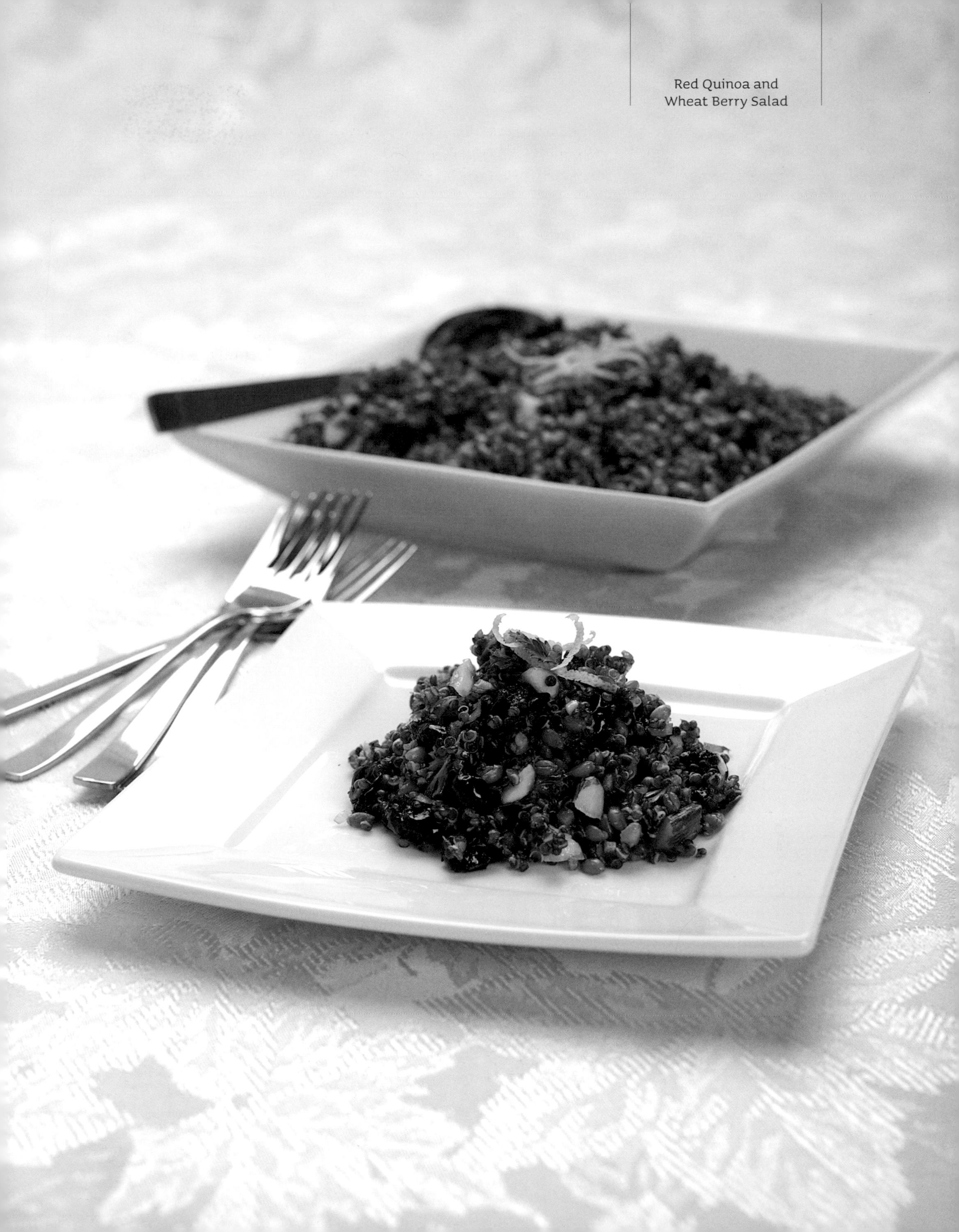

Red Quinoa and
Wheat Berry Salad

This is a variation on the classic Italian *panzanella*—the traditional bread salad. You can either eat this right away, when the bread is very crunchy, or you can refrigerate it and serve it the next day, when the bread is soft and has soaked up the flavours.

Grilled Sourdough and Tomatoes "Panzanella"

4 cups (1 L)	torn or chopped sourdough bread (about one 7 oz/200 g loaf)
¼ cup (60 mL)	extra virgin olive oil, divided
1½ cups (375 mL)	cooked quinoa made with vegetable broth (see pages 5–6)
2 Tbsp (30 mL)	freshly squeezed lemon juice
2 Tbsp (30 mL)	red wine vinegar
6	ripe medium tomatoes (about 1½ lb/750 g), cut into eights (see sidebar)
1½ cups (375 mL)	coarsely chopped English cucumber, peel on (about half a large cucumber)
1	small red onion, thinly sliced
3	cloves garlic, minced
½ cup (125 mL)	drained pimiento-stuffed green olives, cut in halves
½ cup (125 mL)	loosely packed fresh basil, chiffonade (see page 8)
3 Tbsp (45 mL)	coarsely chopped flat-leaf parsley
	Freshly ground black pepper to taste

1. Preheat your outdoor grill or inside broiler. Slice the bread into 1-inch (2.5 cm) slices. Brush slices on both sides with a bit of olive oil. Place on a baking sheet and broil or grill on both sides until well toasted and browned. The bread should be completely dry and crisp. Cool and cut or tear into bite-sized pieces. Alternatively, brush the bread slices with a bit of the oil and cut into bite-sized pieces, then toast in a frying pan over medium heat until browned. Place bread in a large bowl.

2. Add the cooked quinoa and toss well. Sprinkle with the lemon juice and vinegar and toss well so the bread has a chance to absorb the flavours.

3. Add the tomatoes, cucumber, onion, garlic, olives, basil and parsley and toss gently to blend.

4. Drizzle any remaining olive oil over the salad. Sprinkle with freshly ground pepper and toss once more.

5. **TO SERVE:** Taste and adjust the seasonings, if necessary. Let stand at room temperature for 15 minutes before serving.

Makes about 8 cups (2 L) • One serving = 1 cup (250 mL)

The tomatoes should be really ripe for use in this recipe. To avoid the salad from becoming too wet, drain the tomatoes before adding.

Nutrition per serving

309 calories	10 g total fat	1 g saturated fat
0 mg cholesterol	302 mg sodium	47 g carbohydrates
6 g fibre	6 g sugars	9 g protein

Excellent source of folate.

This salad is a great option for brunch, a picnic or your next big family gathering when you want to add a vegetarian dish to the menu. For variety, swap toasted pine nuts or walnuts for the almonds, or use cranberries for the cherries.

YEAR ROUND

Teresa Makarewicz, PHEc

Potluck Party Salad

1. In a large non-stick frying pan, heat the oil over medium heat. Add the garlic, celery and carrots. Stirring occasionally, sauté for 5 to 7 minutes, or until the vegetables are tender. Remove from heat.

2. In a large serving bowl, gently toss the cooked quinoa, vegetable mixture, nuts, seeds and cherries. Toss in the green onions and crumbled feta.

3. **TO SERVE:** Serve immediately or cover and refrigerate. Store in the fridge for up to 2 days.

Makes 8 cups (2 L) • One serving = 1 cup (250 mL)

1 Tbsp (15 mL)	canola oil
3	cloves garlic, minced
2	celery stalks, cut into thirds and julienned (see page 8)
2	medium carrots, scrubbed well, julienned (see page 8)
3 cups (750 mL)	cooked quinoa made with vegetable broth (see pages 5–6)
⅓ cup (80 mL)	whole almonds, chopped
⅓ cup (80 mL)	unsalted pumpkin or sunflower seeds
⅓ cup (80 mL)	dried cherries
7	green onions, thinly sliced
⅔ cup (160 mL)	crumbled goat feta

Nutrition per serving

236 calories	12 g total fat	3 g saturated fat
11 mg cholesterol	289 mg sodium	26 g carbohydrates
4 g fibre	6 g sugars	8 g protein

Excellent source of magnesium and iron.

For rookie curry lovers, this nutrient-dense and colourful salad pairs well with any chickpea dish. Choose a sweeter apple for a more rounded flavour note. Suggestions include Honeycrisp, Cortland or Ambrosia.

Curried Quinoa with Raisins and Apples

1	large red-skinned apple, scrubbed well, cored and chopped into bite-sized pieces (see recipe introduction)
⅓ cup (80 mL)	minced fresh parsley
¼ cup (60 mL)	raisins
¼ cup (60 mL)	coarsely chopped almonds
3	green onions, thinly sliced
2 Tbsp (30 mL)	extra virgin olive oil
½ tsp (2 mL)	curry powder
¼ tsp (1 mL)	ground turmeric (see sidebar page 68)
½ tsp (2 mL)	freshly ground black pepper
2 Tbsp (30 mL)	apple cider vinegar
3 cups (750 mL)	cooked quinoa made with water (see pages 5–6)
¼ cup (60 mL)	0% fat Greek-style yogurt

1. In a large bowl, toss together the apple, parsley, raisins, almonds and green onions.

2. In a small saucepan, warm the oil, curry, turmeric and pepper for 1 to 2 minutes over low heat. Remove from heat and cool for 1 minute. Add the vinegar and pour this mixture over the apple mixture. Toss well.

3. **TO SERVE:** Add the cooked quinoa and toss. Add the yogurt and toss until all ingredients are well coated. Serve immediately.

Makes 4 cups (1 L) • One serving = ½ cup (125 mL)

Nutrition per serving

153 calories	7 g total fat	1 g saturated fat
0 mg cholesterol	74 mg sodium	21 g carbohydrates
3 g fibre	6 g sugars	4 g protein

An excellent source of iron, this colourful side salad will give any athlete an added boost of nutrients. Other optional ingredients to add include steamed asparagus or broccoli and chopped toasted walnuts or other nuts.

SPRING and SUMMER

Carolyn Frail, PHEc

Athlete's Toasted Quinoa Salad

1. In a large saucepan or Dutch oven, toast the quinoa over low heat, stirring constantly, at least 8 to 10 minutes, or until lightly toasted or golden tan in colour.

2. Add the broth and bring to a boil. Reduce heat to medium-low and cook covered for 15 to 20 minutes. The quinoa is done when the grains are translucent and all the liquid has been absorbed. Fluff with a fork, remove from heat and add the raisins. Let stand covered for 5 to 10 minutes, and allow the steam to soften the raisins.

3. Remove the lid and let cool for 10 minutes.

4. Place the cooled quinoa in a large bowl. Add the chickpeas, carrot, parsley, lemon juice and oil. Gently toss together.

5. **TO SERVE:** Refrigerate for up to 4 hours to allow flavours to blend before serving.

Makes 10 cups (2.5 L) • One serving = 1 cup (250 mL)

1½ cups (375 mL)	quinoa, rinsed and drained
2¾ cups (685 mL)	vegetable broth
½ cup (125 mL)	raisins
1 can (14 oz/398 mL)	chickpeas, well rinsed and drained
1	large carrot, scrubbed well and coarsely grated
½ cup (125 mL)	chopped fresh parsley
¼ cup (60 mL)	fresh lemon juice (about 1 large lemon)
2 Tbsp (30 mL)	extra virgin olive oil

Nutrition per serving

201 calories	5 g total fat	1 g saturated fat
0 mg cholesterol	144 mg sodium	34 g carbohydrates
4 g fibre	7 g sugars	6 g protein

Excellent source of iron.

Raw Foods Salad

Fans of raw foods: this is the salad for you. Combining apples, walnuts and mixed greens, it has a spoonful of heart health in every bite. For more walnut flavour, use walnut oil instead of extra virgin olive oil in the salad dressing. NOTE: You need to soak the quinoa overnight before you start the recipe.

FALL and **WINTER**

Bailey Rafferty, SHEA
student member

Raw Foods Salad

1. Place the quinoa in a small bowl and add the water. Cover and refrigerate for 12 to 16 hours. Drain and thoroughly rinse. Set aside to drain.

2. **DRESSING:** In a large bowl, whisk together the oil and vinegar. Add the cinnamon and whisk in well.

3. Toss in the apple, raisins, carrots and walnuts. Toss until all ingredients are well coated.

4. **TO SERVE:** Add the drained quinoa and toss well. Add the mixed greens and toss until the leaves are coated with the dressing. Divide equally between four bowls, add pepper to taste and serve immediately.

Makes 7 cups (1.75 L) • One serving = 1¾ cups (435 mL)

½ cup (125 mL)	quinoa, rinsed and drained
1 cup (250 mL)	water
1	large sweet apple, like a Honeycrisp, chopped into bite-sized pieces
¼ cup (60 mL)	raisins
¼ cup (60 mL)	diced carrots
¼ cup (60 mL)	chopped walnuts
4 cups (1 L)	mixed greens
	Freshly ground black pepper to taste

DRESSING

2 Tbsp (30 mL)	extra virgin olive oil
2 Tbsp (30 mL)	balsamic vinegar
1 tsp (5 mL)	cinnamon

Nutrition per serving

257 calories	13 g total fat	2 g saturated fat
0 mg cholesterol	22 mg sodium	34 g carbohydrates
4 g fibre	12 g sugars	5 g protein

This quick and easy salad can be made most of the year using either fresh or hothouse peppers from Canada. Try serving it with grilled portobello mushrooms or tofu.

Lime Cilantro Salad with Peppers

3 cups (750 mL)	cooked quinoa made with vegetable broth (see pages 5–6)
1	medium red pepper, diced
1	medium orange pepper, diced
¼ cup (60 mL)	fresh cilantro, chopped (more if desired)

DRESSING

Zest of 1	lime
2½ Tbsp (37 mL)	fresh lime juice
2 Tbsp (30 mL)	extra virgin olive oil
1 tsp (5 mL)	liquid honey
	Freshly ground black pepper to taste

1. In a large bowl, toss together the cooked quinoa, red pepper, orange pepper and cilantro.

2. **DRESSING:** In a small bowl, whisk together the lime zest and juice, oil, honey and pepper.

3. **TO SERVE:** Pour the dressing over the quinoa mixture. Toss salad and refrigerate for at least 2 hours before serving.

Makes about 4 cups (1 L) · One serving = ¾ cup (185 mL)

Nutrition per serving

174 calories	7 g total fat	1 g saturated fat
0 mg cholesterol	142 mg sodium	26 g carbohydrates
3 g fibre	3 g sugars	5 g protein

Excellent source of vitamin C and magnesium.

We all need to eat more antioxidant-packed broccoli. This lightly sweet salad is a great way to add this veggie superstar to your day.

FALL and **WINTER**

Linda Lichtenberger, PHEc

Broccoli Salad with Fruit

1. In a large bowl, toss together the broccoli, grapes and orange. Add the cooked quinoa and toss.

2. **DRESSING:** In a small bowl, whisk together the mayonnaise and orange juice.

3. **TO SERVE:** Pour the dressing over the salad ingredients and toss gently. Sprinkle with nuts or seeds if using and serve immediately.

Makes 3½ cups (875 mL) • One serving = ½ cup (125 mL) (without nuts or seeds garnish)

1½ cups (375 mL)	chopped broccoli florets (about 4 large florets)
12	red seedless grapes, cut in half
1	orange, peeled and cut into bite-sized pieces
1½ cups (375 mL)	cooked quinoa made with vegetable broth (see pages 5–6)

DRESSING

¼ cup (60 mL)	low-fat mayonnaise
2 Tbsp (30 mL)	orange juice
2 Tbsp (30 mL)	chopped almonds or whole sunflower seeds for garnish (optional)

Nutrition per serving

94 calories	3 g total fat	0 g saturated fat
3 mg cholesterol	124 mg sodium	14 g carbohydrates
2 g fibre	3 g sugars	2 g protein

Oranges and beets are incredible together: the sweetness from the oranges really rounds out the earthy flavour from the beets. This side salad goes well with grilled tofu with Asian flavours.

Toasted Quinoa Salad with Roasted Beets and Oranges

3	beets (about 12 oz/375 g)
1 cup (250 mL)	quinoa, rinsed and well drained
1 cup (250 mL)	orange juice
½ cup (125 mL)	vegetable broth
1	large clove garlic, minced
1	orange, peeled and chopped into bite-sized pieces, about the size of a walnut
⅓ cup (80 mL)	crumbled goat feta
2 Tbsp (30 mL)	chopped fresh mint
2 Tbsp (30 mL)	chopped fresh parsley

DRESSING

2 Tbsp (30 mL)	extra virgin olive oil
2 Tbsp (30 mL)	sherry or red wine vinegar
2 tsp (10 mL)	Dijon mustard

1. Preheat the oven to 400°F (200°C). Wrap the beets loosely in foil and roast in the oven or in a toaster oven for about 1 hour, or until a knife inserted into the beet comes out easily. Set aside until cool enough to handle. Skin the beets and chop them into pieces about the size of a walnut. Set aside. This step can be done the day before and the beets stored in the fridge.

2. In a large non-stick frying pan over medium-high heat, toast the quinoa, stirring frequently, for about 6 to 10 minutes, or until it is fragrant and begins to snap and pop. (Make sure that most of the quinoa is snapping and popping, not just a couple of seeds.)

3. Add the orange juice, broth and garlic to the pan. Bring to a boil. Reduce heat to low and simmer covered for 15 to 20 minutes, or until all the liquid has been absorbed. Remove from heat and let stand covered for 5 minutes.

4. Using a fork, fluff the quinoa and transfer into a large bowl. Let cool slightly. Add the chopped beets, orange and feta and toss gently.

5. **DRESSING:** In a small bowl, whisk together the oil, vinegar and Dijon mustard. Pour over the quinoa mixture.

6. **TO SERVE:** Add the mint and parsley and toss gently to coat all the ingredients. Serve immediately.

Makes 7 cups (1.75 L) • One serving = 1 cup (250 mL)

Nutrition per serving

187 calories	7 g total fat	2 g saturated fat
7 mg cholesterol	187 mg sodium	27 g carbohydrates
3 g fibre	7 g sugars	5 g protein

Excellent source of folate.

Serve this side salad either warm for a sit-down dinner or chilled over a bed of spring greens in a packed lunch.

YEAR ROUND

Astrid Muschalla, PHEc

Mixed Veggie and Herb Salad

1. In a large saucepan, combine the quinoa, lentils and water. Bring to a boil, then reduce heat to medium-low and cook covered for 18 to 20 minutes, or until the lentils are tender but not mushy. Remove from heat and let stand 5 to 10 minutes. If any water remains, drain the mixture well. Set aside to cool.

2. Meanwhile, in a large bowl, toss together the garlic, green onion, tomato, carrots and cucumber. Add the quinoa and lentils and toss well.

3. **DRESSING:** In a small bowl, whisk together the oil, lime juice, chili powder and cumin. Pour over the quinoa mixture and toss well.

4. **TO SERVE:** Add the parsley and cilantro and toss gently. Serve either slightly warm or refrigerate for 1 hour before serving. Keeps well in the fridge for up to 2 days.

Makes 4 cups (1 L) • One serving = 1 cup (250 mL)

½ cup (125 mL)	quinoa, rinsed and drained
⅓ cup (80 mL)	small dried brown lentils, rinsed and drained
1¾ cups (435 mL)	water
1	clove garlic, minced
1	green onion, chopped
1	tomato, seeded and diced
1	medium carrot, scrubbed well and coarsely grated
1 cup (250 mL)	English cucumber, peel on, diced

DRESSING

1 Tbsp (15 mL)	extra virgin olive oil
2 Tbsp (30 mL)	fresh lime juice
1 tsp (5 mL)	chili powder
½ tsp (2 mL)	ground cumin
¼ cup (60 mL)	finely chopped fresh parsley
¼ cup (60 mL)	finely chopped fresh cilantro

Nutrition per serving

153 calories	5 g total fat	1 g saturated fat
0 mg cholesterol	56 mg sodium	23 g carbohydrates
5 g fibre	3 g sugars	5 g protein

This light dinner is perfect for those hot summer months when it's too hot to be in the kitchen. Edamame or baby green soybeans have a mild flavour and offer a great source of protein along with the quinoa.

fresh Soy B.

Quinoa and Edamame Salad with Asian Flavours

1 cup (250 mL)	quinoa, rinsed and drained
2 cups (500 mL)	vegetable broth
1½ cups (375 mL)	frozen, shelled edamame (see sidebar page 72)
1	red pepper, diced
2	medium carrots, scrubbed well and diced
3	green onions, sliced

DRESSING

2 Tbsp (30 mL)	canola oil
2 Tbsp (30 mL)	rice wine vinegar, no salt or sugar added
2 Tbsp (30 mL)	sodium-reduced soy sauce
1 Tbsp (15 mL)	minced or grated fresh ginger
1 tsp (5 mL)	wasabi paste
Pinch	pepper

With carrots available virtually all year round and hothouse peppers available before and after field peppers, this salad can be an all-season dish. You can also vary the vegetables depending on the season or what you have in your crisper.

1. In an 8-cup (2 L) round, preferably deep microwave dish, combine the quinoa and broth. Cover and microwave at High (100%) for 5 minutes to bring to a boil, then at 60% for 10 to 12 minutes, or until the liquid has been absorbed. Fluff with a fork and let stand covered for 5 minutes.

2. In a microwaveable bowl, combine the edamame with 2 Tbsp (30 mL) of water. Cover and microwave at High for 3 to 4 minutes, or until bright green and tender. Drain.

3. In a large bowl, toss together the cooked quinoa, edamame, red pepper, carrots and green onions.

4. **DRESSING:** In a small bowl, whisk together the oil, vinegar, soy sauce, ginger, wasabi and pepper.

5. **TO SERVE:** Pour the dressing over the quinoa and vegetables and toss well to coat all the ingredients. Serve immediately. Refrigerate any leftovers for up to 2 days.

Makes 6 cups (1.5 L) • One serving = 1½ cups (375 mL)

Nutrition per serving

343 calories	13 g total fat	1 g saturated fat
0 mg cholesterol	579 mg sodium	45 g carbohydrates
8 g fibre	12 g sugars	13 g protein

Excellent source of vitamins A and C.

YEAR ROUND

Joan Chatfield, OHEA
corresponding member

This sweet and crunchy salad has a mild curry flavour, which makes it perfect for anyone who is taking baby steps into the curry world and its health benefits. Packed with dried fruit, this dish is also an excellent source of iron. Serve with either a glass of orange juice or another food rich in vitamin C to enhance iron absorption. NOTE: Look for dried mango in the produce aisle or international food aisle at a larger grocery store.

Curried Fruit and and Nut Salad

1 Tbsp (15 mL)	canola oil
½ tsp (2 mL)	curry powder
½ tsp (2 mL)	turmeric (see sidebar)
1 cup (250 mL)	quinoa, rinsed and drained
2 cups (500 mL)	vegetable broth
½ cup (125 mL)	dried mango, diced
½ cup (125 mL)	dry-roasted whole almonds or cashews
½ cup (125 mL)	dried cranberries
1	large Granny Smith apple, scrubbed well, cored and diced

DRESSING

1 Tbsp (15 mL)	extra virgin olive oil
2 Tbsp (30 mL)	fresh lemon juice
1	clove garlic, minced
1 tsp (5 mL)	grainy Dijon mustard
1 Tbsp (15 mL)	minced fresh parsley

Curcumin, the active ingredient in turmeric, may ease inflammation. Some research suggests that the anti-inflammatory properties turmeric displays may help in the battle against rheumatoid arthritis, heart disease, Alzheimer's and perhaps cancer.

1. Heat a large saucepan over medium heat. Add the oil, curry powder and turmeric. Heat while stirring for 1 to 2 minutes. Add the quinoa and sauté for about another minute.

2. Add the broth and bring to a boil. Reduce heat to medium-low and simmer covered for 15 to 20 minutes. The quinoa is done when the grains are translucent and most of the liquid has been absorbed.

3. Fluff with a fork, remove from heat and let stand for 5 to 10 minutes. To speed up cooling, spread the cooked quinoa on a clean, dry baking sheet and let sit until completely cooled.

4. **DRESSING:** Meanwhile, in a large bowl, whisk together the oil, lemon juice, garlic, Dijon mustard and parsley. Toss in the mango, almonds or cashews, cranberries and apple.

5. **TO SERVE:** Add the cooled quinoa and toss gently until well combined. Serve immediately and refrigerate any leftovers up to 1 day.

Makes 6 cups (1.5 L) • One serving = 1½ cups (375 mL)

Nutrition per serving

474 calories	19 g total fat	2 g saturated fat
0 mg cholesterol	399 mg sodium	70 g carbohydrates
8 g fibre	29 g sugars	10 g protein

Excellent source of iron.

With the convenience of frozen vegetables, this easy dinner for two is ready in about 25 minutes, start to finish. Don't skip the toasting step, as it really helps bring out the nutlike flavour of the quinoa.

WINTER

Ellie Topp, PHEc

Winter Salad with Toasted Quinoa

½ cup (125 mL)	quinoa, rinsed and drained
¾ cup (185 mL)	vegetable broth
2 tsp (10 mL)	sodium-reduced soy sauce
½ cup (125 mL)	frozen corn
½ cup (125 mL)	thinly sliced carrots, scrubbed well, peel left on
1 cup (250 mL)	small frozen peas
4	leaves romaine or other dark-leafed lettuce or 2 cups (500 mL) baby spinach
2 Tbsp (30 mL)	chopped pistachio or cashew nuts, unsalted
1	tomato, sliced into wedges, for garnish

1. In a small saucepan over medium heat, toast the quinoa, stirring frequently, for about 4 to 6 minutes, until it begins to snap and is slightly toasted.

2. Add the broth and soy sauce. Bring to a boil, then reduce heat to low and simmer covered for 10 minutes. Stir in the corn and carrots. Return to a boil, then reduce heat to low and simmer covered for another 5 to 8 minutes, or until the vegetables are tender-crisp and all the liquid has been absorbed.

3. Rinse the peas in hot water to defrost. Drain the peas and stir into the quinoa mixture. Refrigerate or proceed to the next step.

4. **TO SERVE:** Place 2 lettuce leaves on each plate or 1 cup (250 mL) of the baby spinach. Mound the quinoa in the centre. Sprinkle each serving with 1 Tbsp (15 mL) of the nuts and garnish with tomato wedges.

Makes 2⅓ cups (660 mL) • One serving = 1⅓ cups (330 mL)

Nutrition per serving

326 calories	7 g total fat	1 g saturated fat
0 mg cholesterol	469 mg sodium	55 g carbohydrates
10 g fibre	10 g sugars	13 g protein

Excellent source of vitamin A, folate and iron.

Red Quinoa and Lentil
Salad with Apples
and Walnuts

This high-protein, all-in-one main course salad is chock-full of fibre and B vitamins. The added heart-healthy benefits of apples and pomegranate seeds make this salad super nutritious as well as a fabulous-tasting entrée. A little goes a long way.

FALL and **WINTER**

Cristina Fernandes, PHEc

Red Quinoa and Lentil Salad with Apples and Walnuts

1. In a large bowl, toss together the cooked quinoa, apples, green onion, lentils, walnuts and pomegranate seeds.

2. **DRESSING:** In a small bowl, whisk together the oil, vinegar, cinnamon and red pepper flakes.

3. **TO SERVE:** Drizzle the dressing over the salad and toss gently to coat all the ingredients evenly. Serve immediately.

Makes 10 cups (2.5 L) • **One serving = 1 cup (250 mL)**

5 cups (1.25 L)	cooked red quinoa made with water (see pages 5–6)
2	medium Gala or Fuji or Braeburn apples, cut into bite-sized pieces
⅓ cup (80 mL)	chopped green onion
1 can (19 oz/540 mL)	lentils, well rinsed and drained
½ cup (125 mL)	coarsely chopped walnuts
1 cup (250 mL)	pomegranate seeds or 1 pomegranate, seeded (see page 9)

DRESSING

2 Tbsp (30 mL)	extra virgin olive oil
2 Tbsp (30 mL)	balsamic vinegar
½ tsp (2 mL)	ground cinnamon
¼ tsp (1 mL)	hot pepper flakes

Nutrition per serving

466 calories	11 g total fat	1 g saturated fat
0 mg cholesterol	79 mg sodium	79 g carbohydrates
13 g fibre	11 g sugars	15 g protein

Excellent source of riboflavin, folate, magnesium and iron.

With so many beautiful colours, this salad has eye *and* taste appeal. NOTE: To cook frozen edamame, follow package directions, omitting the salt.

Red and Green Salad with Edamame

DRESSING

2 Tbsp (30 mL)	extra virgin olive oil
3 Tbsp (45 mL)	fresh lime juice
1 Tbsp (15 mL)	liquid honey
1 tsp (5 mL)	minced fresh ginger
1	clove garlic, minced

SALAD

1 cup (250 mL)	frozen shelled edamame, cooked and cooled (see recipe introduction)
½ cup (125 mL)	radishes, cut into quarters and thinly sliced
½ cup (125 mL)	dried cranberries
2	green onions, sliced
3 cups (750 mL)	cooked quinoa made with vegetable broth (see pages 5–6)
¼ cup (60 mL)	whole raw almonds, coarsely chopped, for garnish

1. **DRESSING:** In a small bowl, whisk together the oil, lime juice, honey, ginger and garlic.

2. In a large bowl, toss together the edamame, radishes, cranberries and green onions. Pour the dressing over the edamame mixture and toss.

3. Add the quinoa and gently toss until the mixture is well blended. Sprinkle with almonds and serve immediately.

Makes 5 cups (1.25 L) • One serving = 1 cup (250 mL)

You can buy edamame in the frozen food section of larger grocery stores, where you can choose either in the pod or shelled (as for this recipe). Or check out your local farmer's market for fresh edamame.

Nutrition per serving

324 calories	13 g total fat	2 g saturated fat
0 mg cholesterol	177 mg sodium	45 g carbohydrates
5 g fibre	14 g sugars	10 g protein

Excellent source of magnesium and iron.

Combining lentils with quinoa not only bumps up the protein count, it also adds a new flavour element to this take on a traditional tabbouleh salad.

"Tabbouleh" with Lentils

1. In a large bowl, toss together the lentils, cucumber, red onion, mint and parsley.

2. **DRESSING:** In a small bowl, whisk together the lemon zest, juice, oil and pepper. Pour over the lentil mixture and toss until ingredients are well coated.

3. **TO SERVE:** Add the cooked quinoa and toss until combined. Serve immediately.

Makes 8 cups (2 L) • One serving = 2 cups (500 mL)

1 can (19 oz/540 mL)	lentils, well rinsed and drained
1½ cups (375 mL)	diced seedless cucumber, peel on
¾ cup (185 mL)	finely diced red onion
1 cup (250 mL)	fresh mint, chiffonade (see page 8)
1 cup (250 mL)	coarsely chopped flat-leaf parsley
3 cups (750 mL)	cooked quinoa made with vegetable broth (see pages 5–6)
DRESSING	
Zest of 1	large lemon
¼ cup + 2 Tbsp (90 mL)	fresh lemon juice (about 1 large lemon)
2 Tbsp (30 mL)	extra virgin olive oil
¼ tsp (1 mL)	freshly ground black pepper, or to taste

Nutrition per serving

346 calories	11 g total fat	1 g saturated fat
0 mg cholesterol	395 mg sodium	53 g carbohydrates
9 g fibre	4 g sugars	14 g protein

Excellent source of folate, vitamin C, magnesium and iron.

SUMMER

Grace Warmels, SHEA
student member

A crowd-pleaser for any big family function, this salad *tastes* like summer. The red quinoa gives the dish extra crunch and a great colour. NOTE: We saved the mint to use as a garnish (see photo), but feel free to toss it into the salad.

Sweet Summer Red Quinoa Salad

DRESSING

2 Tbsp (30 mL)	extra virgin olive oil
Zest of 1	lemon
2 Tbsp (30 mL)	fresh lemon juice
2 tsp (10 mL)	ground cumin
2	cloves garlic, minced

SALAD

1 can (19 oz/540 mL)	black beans, well rinsed and drained
1¾ cups (435 mL)	frozen corn, thawed (see sidebar page 124)
1	large ripe avocado, peeled, pitted and diced
½	red onion, diced
1	large red pepper, chopped
¾ cup (185 mL)	grape tomatoes, halved
1	orange, peel cut off and fruit cut into small pieces
3 cups (750 mL)	cooked red quinoa made with vegetable broth (see pages 5–6)
⅓ cup (80 mL)	chopped fresh parsley
1 Tbsp (15 mL)	fresh mint, chiffonade (see page 8)
¼ tsp (1 mL)	freshly ground black pepper

1. **DRESSING:** In a large bowl, whisk together the oil, lemon zest and juice, cumin and garlic.

2. **SALAD:** Add the beans, corn, avocado, red onion, red pepper, grape tomatoes and orange and gently toss.

3. Add the cooked quinoa, parsley, mint and pepper and gently toss until combined.

4. **TO SERVE:** Refrigerate for at least 2 hours and serve chilled. Salad keeps up to 3 days in the fridge—if there *are* any leftovers.

Makes 10 cups (2.5 L) • One serving = 2 cups (500 mL)

Nutrition per serving

339 calories	13 g total fat	2 g saturated fat
0 mg cholesterol	169 mg sodium	48 g carbohydrates
11 g fibre	11 g sugars	11 g protein

Excellent source of vitamin C.

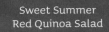

Andrea Villneff, OHEA
provisional member

A hot salad? Oh, yeah! And if you love mango combined with the flavours of curry and cumin, you are going to love this salad.

Mango, Pepper and Tofu Hot Salad

1 cup (250 mL)	red quinoa, rinsed and drained
2 cups (500 mL)	vegetable broth
2 Tbsp (30 mL)	canola oil, divided
1	ripe mango, diced
1	red pepper, diced
½	English cucumber, peel on, diced
½ tsp (2 mL)	ground cumin
½ tsp (2 mL)	curry powder
1 tsp (5 mL)	freshly ground black pepper
3 Tbsp (45 mL)	fresh lemon juice
1 Tbsp (15 mL)	finely chopped fresh cilantro
1 lb (500 g)	extra-firm tofu, cut into 1-inch (2.5 cm) cubes

1. Place the quinoa in a large saucepan, add the broth and bring to a boil. Reduce heat to medium-low and simmer covered for 15 to 20 minutes. The quinoa is done when the grains are translucent and all the liquid has been absorbed. Fluff with a fork, remove from heat and let stand covered for 5 to 10 minutes.

2. Heat a large frying pan over medium heat. Add 1 Tbsp (15 mL) of the oil, and the mango, red pepper and cucumber. Sauté for 2 to 3 minutes, or until the red pepper is still slightly crunchy.

3. Add the cumin and curry powder and sauté for another minute. Add the black pepper and lemon juice. Mix well. Remove from heat and transfer to a large bowl. Gently fold in the cooked quinoa and cilantro.

4. Add the remaining 1 Tbsp (15 mL) of oil to a frying pan. Fry the tofu 5 to 7 minutes, until golden brown.

5. **TO SERVE:** Add the tofu to the quinoa mixture, toss gently and serve immediately.

Makes 8 cups (2 L) • One serving = 2 cups (500 mL)

Nutrition per serving

265 calories	15 g total fat	2 g saturated fat
0 mg cholesterol	365 mg sodium	19 g carbohydrates
4 g fibre	11 g sugars	15 g protein
Excellent source of vitamin C.		

Great for university students, this all-in-one-bowl meal can be made the night before so the flavours can really blend together. It's great for a picnic or a buffet as well.

SPRING and **SUMMER**

Joyce Ho, OHEA
student member

Quick Meal-in-a-Bowl Salad

1. In a large bowl, gently toss together the lentils, orange pepper, tomatoes, shallot, cooked quinoa and avocado.

2. **DRESSING:** In a small bowl, whisk together the lemon juice, vinegar and oil. Pour over the salad and gently toss.

3. **TO SERVE:** Add the lemon zest and pepper and toss well. Serve immediately or store in the fridge for up to 3 days.

Makes 6 cups (1.5 L) • One serving = 1 cup (250 mL)

1 can (19 oz/540 mL)	lentils, well rinsed and drained
1	orange pepper, diced
1½ cups (325 mL)	grape tomatoes, halved
1	shallot, minced
3 cups (750 mL)	cooked red quinoa made with water (see pages 5–6)
1	large ripe avocado, peeled, pitted and diced
Zest of 1	lemon
¼ tsp (1 mL)	freshly ground black pepper, or to taste

DRESSING

4–5 Tbsp (60–75 mL)	fresh lemon juice, or to taste
2 Tbsp (30 mL)	sherry vinegar
2 Tbsp (30 mL)	extra virgin olive oil

Nutrition per serving

298 calories	12 g total fat	2 g saturated fat
0 mg cholesterol	16 mg sodium	40 g carbohydrates
10 g fibre	4 g sugars	12 g protein

Excellent source of vitamin C.

Ideal for potlucks and picnics, this colourful salad has enough protein to be served as a vegetarian main course. For even more colour plus some added texture, try using red quinoa.

Curried Chickpea Salad

1 can (19 oz/540 mL)	chickpeas, well rinsed and drained
2	celery stalks, thinly sliced
2	green onions, thinly sliced
1	red pepper, julienned (see page 8)
½ cup (125 mL)	chopped fresh parsley
3 cups (750 mL)	cooked quinoa made with vegetable broth (see pages 5–6)

DRESSING

2 Tbsp (30 mL)	chopped onion (about ¼ of a medium onion)
2 Tbsp (30 mL)	canola oil
2 Tbsp (30 mL)	apple cider vinegar
2 Tbsp (30 mL)	brown sugar, packed
1	clove garlic, minced
1 tsp (5 mL)	curry powder
¼ tsp (1 mL)	freshly ground black pepper

1. In a large bowl, toss together the chickpeas, celery, green onions, red pepper and parsley. Add the cooked quinoa and toss. Cover and refrigerate for at least 2 hours.

2. **DRESSING:** Meanwhile, using a food processor or immersion blender, purée the onion, oil, vinegar, brown sugar, garlic, curry powder and pepper. Pour the dressing into a jar and set aside.

3. Once the salad is chilled, drizzle the dressing over the salad and toss lightly to coat all the ingredients.

4. **TO SERVE:** Serve immediately or cover and refrigerate. Will keep covered in the fridge for up to 2 days.

Makes about 8 cups (2 L) • One serving = 1 cup (250 mL)

Nutrition per serving

384 calories	12 g total fat	1 g saturated fat
0 mg cholesterol	277 mg sodium	60 g carbohydrates
9 g fibre	10 g sugars	13 g protein

Excellent source of vitamin C, folate, magnesium and iron.

Side Dishes

A SIDE DISH IS DEFINED as any dish that is served alongside the main course or entrée. Pilafs, vegetables and technically *fries* would all fit this description. Now, you *will* find recipes for pilafs and veggies in this chapter, but fries? Well, they just weren't healthy enough to make it into this book, although if sweet potato oven fries were made with quinoa, they probably would have. (And the recipe on page 85 is really close.)

All of the tasty sides in this chapter offer great flavour and contain some protein but don't offer enough protein to be considered as the main course in a vegetarian meal.

A light, fresh-tasting appetizer or side dish bursting with flavour, these rolls are great for a buffet at a cocktail party. NOTE: For a more intense flavour, start marinating the tofu up to 24 hours before assembly. Of course, the quinoa too can be made ahead and stored covered in the fridge.

Spring Rolls with Asian-Marinated Tofu

1. **MARINADE FOR TOFU:** In a medium bowl, whisk together the green onions, rice vinegar, oil, soy sauce, honey and chili sauce. Reserve ½ cup (125 mL) and store covered in the fridge. This will be the dipping sauce. Pour the remaining marinade into a large resealable plastic bag or a shallow glass dish. Add the tofu slices and marinate for at least 2 hours, preferably overnight, or up to 24 hours before assembly. (If you are using a shallow dish, cover and refrigerate. If you are using a resealable bag, seal tightly and refrigerate.)

2. **FILLING:** The next day or later the same day, in a medium bowl, whisk together the vinegar and oil. Add the cooked quinoa and green onions and toss to combine. Set aside.

3. Fill a large dish (a large frying pan works well too) with 2 inches (5 cm) of water. Soak one rice paper in the water for 30 to 40 seconds, or until softened. Gently shake off excess liquid.

4. **TO ASSEMBLE:** Spoon about 1 Tbsp (15 mL) of the quinoa filling in the centre of the rice paper. Lay 2 slices of the red pepper, 1 slice of mango, 2 slices of tofu and 1 basil leaf on top of the quinoa. Fold in both sides of the rice paper and roll from the bottom until sealed. Continue to soak and fill the rice papers. Store the assembled rolls in a dish lined and covered with moist paper towel or a tea towel.

5. **TO SERVE:** Serve as soon as all of the rolls have been assembled. Pour the reserved marinade into a small bowl to serve alongside as dipping sauce.

Makes 24 rolls · One serving = 1 roll with 1 tsp (5 mL) dipping sauce

MARINADE FOR TOFU & DIPPING SAUCE

6 Tbsp (90 mL)	finely sliced green onion (about 4)
¼ cup (60 mL)	seasoned rice wine vinegar
2 Tbsp (30 mL)	canola oil
2 Tbsp (30 mL)	low-sodium soy sauce
2 Tbsp (30 mL)	liquid honey
1 Tbsp (15 mL)	Asian or Thai garlic chili sauce
12 oz (360 g)	extra-firm tofu, sliced into forty-eight ½-inch × ½-inch × 2-inch (1 cm × 1 cm × 5 cm) slices

FILLING

2 Tbsp (30 mL)	seasoned rice wine vinegar
1 Tbsp (15 mL)	canola oil
2 cups (500 mL)	cooked quinoa made with water (see pages 5–6)
¼ cup (60 mL)	thinly sliced green onion (about 3)
24 6-inch (15 cm)	rice paper sheets
1	red pepper, cut in ¼-inch (6 mm) slices lengthwise
1	mango, cut in ¼-inch (6 mm) slices lengthwise
24	fresh basil leaves

Nutrition per serving

137 calories	3 g total fat	0 g saturated fat
0 mg cholesterol	76 mg sodium	22 g carbohydrates
2 g fibre	4 g sugars	5 g protein

Double Sesame Quinoa (top) made with white sesame seeds and red quinoa (middle), Saffron Quinoa (bottom) (page 84)

This unique *less is more* recipe is a perfect side dish to Asian-flavoured grilled tofu or shelled edamame. The sesame oil gives this dish a real double hit of sesame flavour.

YEAR ROUND

Margaret Dickenson, PHEc

Double Sesame Quinoa

1. Place the quinoa in a large saucepan, add the water and bring to a boil. Reduce heat to medium-low and cook covered for 15 to 20 minutes. The quinoa is done when the grains are translucent and all the water has been absorbed. Fluff with a fork, remove from heat and let stand covered for 5 to 10 minutes. Remove lid and let cool.

2. If you want to serve this warmer than room temperature, go on to Step 3. If you want a room-temperature version, cool longer. To speed up cooling, spread the cooked quinoa on a clean, dry baking sheet and let sit until completely cooled.

3. Toss the quinoa with the sesame oil and seeds. Season with crushed black peppercorns. Serve immediately or store in the fridge for up to 2 days and serve cold.

Makes about 3 cups (750 mL) · One serving = ½ cup (125 mL)

1 cup (250 mL)	quinoa
1½ cups (375 mL)	water
2 Tbsp (30 mL)	sesame oil
1 Tbsp (15 mL)	black sesame seeds (see sidebar)
1 tsp (5 mL)	crushed black peppercorns, or to taste

If you can't find black sesame seeds, use white and change the quinoa to red for a great colour combo.

Nutrition per serving

155 calories	7 g total fat	1 g saturated fat
0 mg cholesterol	7 mg sodium	20 g carbohydrates
2 g fibre	0 g sugars	4 g protein

Saffron, the world's most expensive spice, is the stigma from a small purple crocus. The stigmas are hand-picked and then dried. With only three stigmas per crocus, it's no wonder this spice is so pricey, but a little goes a really long way. Its buttery flavour and fabulous colour make it a must in this easy yet elegant dish. (See photo on page 82.)

Saffron Quinoa

1¼ cups (310 mL)	vegetable broth
¼ cup (60 mL)	minced fresh parsley
¼ tsp (1 mL)	crushed saffron threads
¼ tsp (1 mL)	freshly ground black pepper
⅔ cup (160 mL)	quinoa, rinsed and drained
2 Tbsp (30 mL)	extra virgin olive oil
4	green onions, finely chopped

1. In a medium saucepan, bring the broth to a boil. Add the parsley, saffron and pepper. Cover, remove from heat and let steep for 5 minutes. Return to a boil and stir well. Add the quinoa. Return to a boil, then reduce heat to medium-low and cook covered for 15 to 20 minutes, or until the quinoa grains are translucent and all the liquid has been absorbed. Fluff with a fork, remove from heat and let stand covered for 5 minutes.

2. Meanwhile, in a small frying pan, heat the oil over medium heat. Add the onions and sauté for about 1 minute.

3. **TO SERVE:** Add the onions to the cooked quinoa, toss gently and serve immediately.

Makes 2 cups (500 mL) · **One serving = ½ cup (125 mL)**

Nutrition per serving

182 calories	9 g total fat	1 g saturated fat
0 mg cholesterol	155 mg sodium	23 g carbohydrates
3 g fibre	1 g sugars	4 g protein

Sweet potatoes are loaded with beta carotene, an antioxidant that can help reduce your chances of developing certain cancers. Any recipe that pairs sweet potatoes with quinoa instantly becomes a health and flavour winner.

FALL and **WINTER**

Jennifer MacKenzie, PHEc

Quinoa with Cumin-Scented Sweet Potatoes

1. Preheat the oven to 450°F (230°C). Line a rimmed baking sheet (9- × 13-inch/23 × 33 cm) with foil or parchment paper.

2. Combine the sweet potatoes, oil, cumin, coriander and pepper on the prepared baking sheet. (Just trying to make your life easier.). Spread out into a single layer and roast for about 20 minutes, stirring once or twice, until the sweet potatoes are golden brown on the outside and tender inside.

3. Meanwhile, place the quinoa in a large saucepan, add the broth and bring to a boil. Reduce heat to medium-low and simmer covered for 15 to 20 minutes, or until the quinoa is translucent and most of the liquid has been absorbed. Fluff with a fork, remove from heat and let stand covered for 5 minutes.

4. Gently fold the sweet potato and lemon juice into the cooked quinoa. Season to taste with pepper.

5. **TO SERVE:** Sprinkle with the almonds and cilantro. Serve with Spinach Roti (page 86) if desired.

Makes about 6 cups (1.5 L) lightly packed • **One serving = 1 cup (250 mL)**

1½ lb (750 g)	sweet potato (about 1 large), peeled and cut into ½-inch (1 cm) cubes
2 Tbsp (30 mL)	extra virgin olive oil
1½ tsp (7 mL)	ground cumin
1 tsp (5 mL)	ground coriander
¼ tsp (1 mL)	freshly ground black pepper
1 cup (250 mL)	quinoa, rinsed and drained
1¾ cups (435 mL)	vegetable broth
2 Tbsp (30 mL)	freshly squeezed lemon or lime juice
2 Tbsp (30 mL)	coarsely chopped almonds
¼ cup (60 mL)	chopped fresh cilantro

Nutrition per serving

285 calories	8 g total fat	1 g saturated fat
0 mg cholesterol	211 mg sodium	48 g carbohydrates
7 g fibre	6 g sugars	7 g protein

Excellent source of vitamin A and iron.

A healthier version of a traditional South Asian flatbread, this roti contains 3 grams of both protein and fibre in each serving. Not bad for a little flatbread. It makes a perfect accompaniment for any curry dish.

Spinach Roti

½ cup (125 mL)	quinoa flour (more if needed) (see page 7)
½ cup (125 mL)	whole wheat flour
½ cup (125 mL)	finely chopped baby spinach
1 tsp (5 mL)	ground cumin
2 tsp (10 mL)	canola oil, divided
¼ cup (60 mL)	warm water (more if needed)

1. In a medium bowl, combine the quinoa and whole wheat flours, chopped spinach, cumin and 1 tsp (5 mL) of the oil.

2. Slowly add the water and knead to make a soft dough. Add extra water if needed.

3. Rub the remaining 1 tsp (5 mL) of oil on the palms of your hands, and then divide the dough into six equal-sized balls, rolling them between your oiled palms.

4. Place the dough balls on a clean counter or cutting board. Using a rolling pin, roll out each ball until very thin, about 6–7 inches (15–18 cm) in diameter. If the dough sticks to the board, dust with extra quinoa flour.

5. Heat a large non-stick frying pan over medium heat. Roast the roti in a dry pan on both sides until golden brown. Alternatively, use an electric tortilla maker.

6. **TO SERVE:** Serve hot with a yogurt and vegetable dip or serve with Curried Quinoa, Sweet Potato and Cauliflower (page 100).

Makes 6 roti • One serving = 1 roti

Nutrition per serving

93 calories	2 g total fat	0 g saturated fat
0 mg cholesterol	10 mg sodium	15 g carbohydrates
3 g fibre	0 g sugars	3 g protein

Make this in the fall when local squash are plentiful. It is a wonderful dish to serve at Thanksgiving. NOTE: To prepare in advance, follow the recipe through Step 3, then cover and refrigerate. An hour before serving time, preheat the oven to 375°F (190°C). Bake for 45 minutes, or until tops are golden.

FALL and **WINTER**

Donna Washburn, PHEc,
& Heather Butt, PHEc

Pecan and Quinoa–Stuffed Squash

1. Preheat the oven to 375°F (190°C). Lightly grease a 9-inch (23 cm) square baking pan with canola oil.

2. Place the quinoa in a small saucepan, add the broth and bring to a boil. Reduce heat to medium-low and cook covered for 15 to 20 minutes. The quinoa is done when the grains are translucent and all the liquid has been absorbed. Fluff with a fork, remove from heat and let stand covered for 5 to 10 minutes.

3. With a small knife, pierce each squash through to the centre in four places. Place one squash on a paper towel in the microwave. Microwave at High for 6 to 8 minutes, turning once, until the squash is tender when pierced with a knife. Remove from the microwave and let stand for 5 minutes. Repeat with the other squash. (Cooking time will depend on the size of the squash.)

4. Cut each squash in half crosswise and remove seeds. Trim a thin slice off the bottom of each so they will lie flat. Place the squash cut side up in the prepared baking pan and set aside.

5. In a large frying pan, heat the olive oil over medium heat. Sauté the celery, onion and sage for 6 to 8 minutes or just until softened. Remove from heat and stir in the parsley, marjoram, salt, pepper and nutmeg. Stir in the cooked quinoa and pecans. Spoon the mixture evenly into the squash halves.

6. Bake for 15 to 20 minutes, or until tops are golden. To make the recipe go further, double the filling recipe and serve the extra as a pilaf another day. (Cook once and serve twice.)

Makes 4 servings • One serving = ½ squash

¼ cup (60 mL)	quinoa, rinsed and drained
¾ cup (185 mL)	vegetable broth
2	small acorn squash
2 tsp (10 mL)	extra virgin olive oil
2	stalks celery, diced
½ cup (125 mL)	chopped onion
1 Tbsp (15 mL)	chopped fresh sage
½ cup (125 mL)	chopped fresh parsley
¾ tsp (4 mL)	dried marjoram leaves
Pinch	salt
¼ tsp (1 mL)	freshly ground black pepper
Pinch	ground nutmeg
½ cup (125 mL)	coarsely chopped pecans

Fresh herbs keep longer if wrapped in a slightly dampened paper towel and placed in a sealed plastic bag in the produce drawer of your fridge.

Nutrition per serving

254 calories	13 g total fat	1 g saturated fat
0 mg cholesterol	98 mg sodium	34 g carbohydrates
6 g fibre	2 g sugars	5 g protein

Excellent source of thiamin and magnesium.

Make this autumn dish as colourful as you want by choosing a rainbow of peppers. NOTE: To increase the protein, use black or small red beans instead of the corn.

Cajun Stuffed Bell Peppers with Tomatoes

1 cup (250 mL)	red quinoa, rinsed and drained
1½ cup (375 mL)	vegetable broth
4	large peppers (choose your favourite colours)
1 Tbsp (15 mL)	canola oil
½	green pepper, diced
½ cup (125 mL)	finely diced shallots (about 2 large)
½ cup (125 mL)	finely diced celery
2	cloves garlic, minced
1 tsp (5 mL)	paprika
1 Tbsp (15 mL)	finely chopped fresh parsley
1 tsp (5 mL)	dried thyme leaves
⅛ tsp (0.5 mL)	cayenne pepper
1 cup (250 mL)	frozen corn (see sidebar page 124)
1 can (14 oz/398 mL)	diced tomatoes, drained, juice reserved
1 cup (250 mL)	tomato sauce, no salt added
¼ cup (60 mL)	fresh parsley sprigs for garnish

1. Place the quinoa in a large saucepan, add the broth and bring to a boil. Reduce heat to medium-low and cook covered for 15 to 20 minutes. The quinoa will be slightly chewy. Fluff with a fork, remove from heat and let stand covered for 5 to 10 minutes.

2. Line a 9- × 13-inch (3.5 L) casserole dish with either foil or wet parchment paper (see page 10).

3. Slice the 4 peppers in half lengthwise through the stem. Remove and discard seeds and membrane.

4. Boil 12 cups (3 L) of water in a large saucepan and cook the pepper halves for 5 minutes in the boiling water. Carefully drain and place the halves cut sides up in the prepared pan. Alternatively, place the pepper halves cut sides down into a microwaveable dish, add 2 Tbsp (30 mL) of water and microwave at High for 3 to 5 minutes, until the peppers have slightly softened.

5. Preheat the oven to 350°F (175°C). In a large non-stick frying pan over medium heat, heat the oil. Sauté the green pepper, shallots, celery and garlic about 3 to 5 minutes, until translucent. Stir in the paprika, parsley, thyme, cayenne pepper, corn and tomatoes.

6. Add the cooked quinoa to the vegetable mixture and stir well.

7. Stuff the pepper halves with all of the stuffing mixture. Pour the reserved tomato juice and tomato sauce into the pan between the peppers. Cover with foil or parchment paper.

8. Bake for 45 minutes, or until the peppers are tender.

9. **TO SERVE:** Pour ¼ cup (60 mL) of the hot tomato juice over each pepper half and garnish with parsley.

Makes 8 large pepper halves • One serving = 1 pepper half

Nutrition per serving

146 calories	3 g total fat	0 g saturated fat
0 mg cholesterol	178 mg sodium	26 g carbohydrates
4 g fibre	7 g sugars	5 g protein

Excellent source of vitamin C.

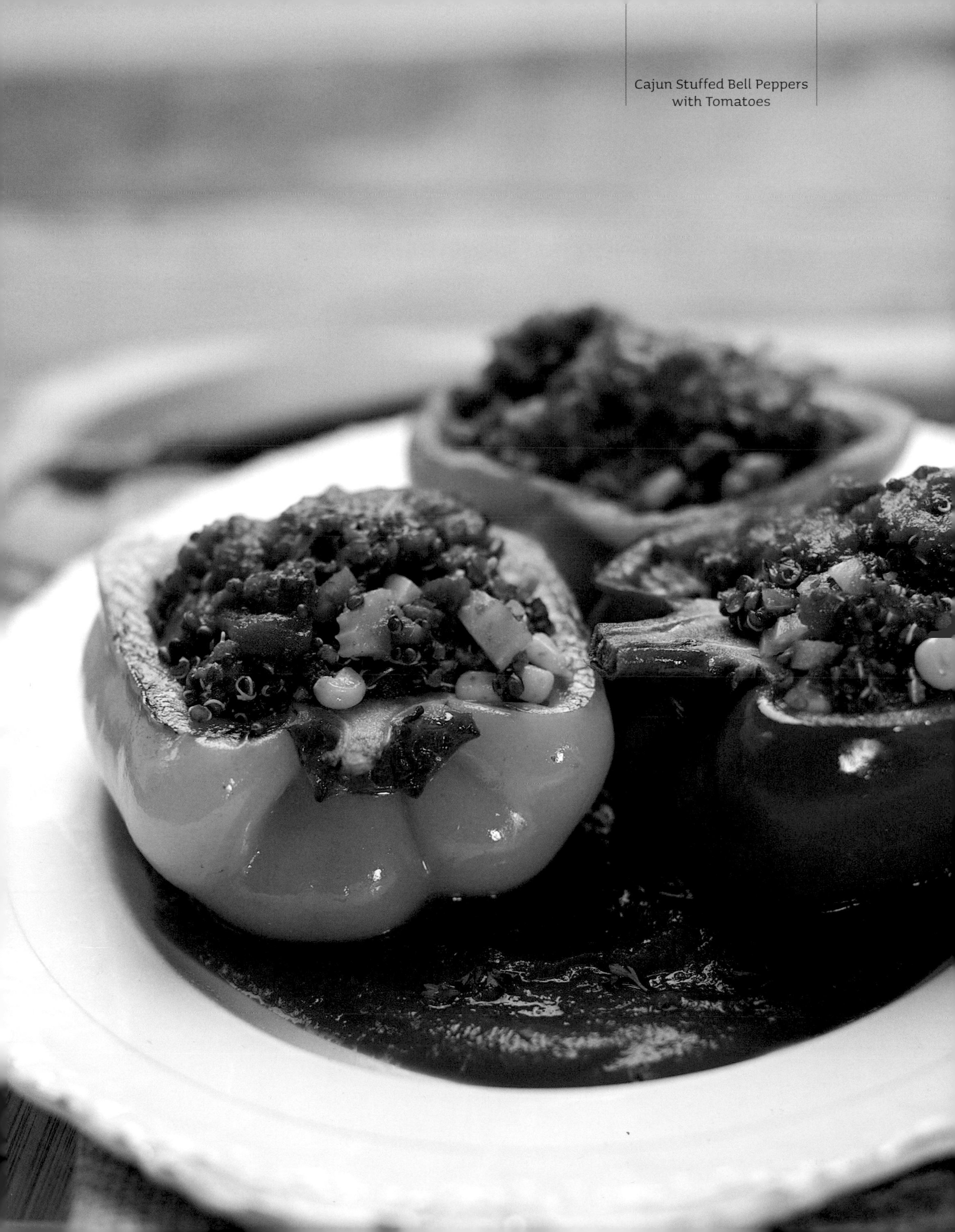

Cajun Stuffed Bell Peppers with Tomatoes

FALL and **WINTER**

Nazima Qureshi, OHEA
student member

This twist on a traditional vegetable biryani is HOT on the spicy-o-meter. It is only for those brave cooks who are willing to go on a very spicy adventure.

Spicy Vegetable "Biryani"

1 cup (250 mL)	quinoa, rinsed and drained
2 cups (500 mL)	vegetable broth
2 Tbsp (30 mL)	canola oil
1	onion, thinly sliced
2 tsp (10 mL)	finely minced ginger
2	cloves garlic, minced
2 tsp (10 mL)	red pepper flakes
½ tsp (2 mL)	turmeric
1 tsp (5 mL)	ground coriander
1 tsp (5 mL)	chili powder
1	large potato (about 5 oz/150 g) peeled and chopped into 1½-inch (4 cm) pieces
2 cups (500 mL)	frozen mixed vegetables (see sidebar page 124)
1 tsp (5 mL)	fresh lemon juice
2 Tbsp (30 mL)	0% fat Greek-style yogurt
¼ cup (60 mL)	chopped cilantro

1. Place the quinoa in a large saucepan, add the broth and bring to a boil. Reduce heat to medium-low and cook covered for 15 to 20 minutes. The quinoa is done when the grains are translucent and all the liquid has been absorbed. Fluff with a fork, remove from heat and let stand covered for 5 to 10 minutes.

2. In a small frying pan, heat the canola oil over medium heat. Sauté the onions about 3 to 6 minutes, until golden brown. Reduce heat to low and add the ginger, garlic, red pepper flakes, turmeric, coriander and chili powder and stir well. You should get a huge hit of fabulous aromas. Remove from heat.

3. In a small saucepan, bring 1 cup (250 mL) of water to a boil. Add the potatoes and cook covered for 8 to 10 minutes, or until the potatoes soften slightly. Do not drain.

4. Add the mixed vegetables and fold in until evenly mixed. Stir in the lemon juice and yogurt. Remove from heat.

5. **TO SERVE:** Fold the potato mixture and the onion mixture into the cooked quinoa. Add the cilantro and serve immediately. Serve with Spinach Roti on page 86 if desired.

Makes 6 cups (1.5 L) • One serving = 1½ cups (375 mL)

Nutrition per serving

311 calories	10 g total fat	1 g saturated fat
0 mg cholesterol	60 mg sodium	48 g carbohydrates
6 g fibre	4 g sugars	9 g protein

Excellent source of vitamin A and magnesium.

Toasting the quinoa adds extra nutty flavours that go really well with the full-bodied taste of the immunity-enhancing shiitake mushrooms.

YEAR ROUND

Teresa Makarewicz, PHEc

Toasted Quinoa and Mushroom Pilaf

1. In a large saucepan over medium heat, heat the oil. Add the mushrooms, shallots, thyme and pepper and sauté for 3 to 5 minutes, or until the onion is just starting to brown and most of the moisture from the mushrooms has evaporated.

2. Add the quinoa and cook, stirring, about 5 minutes, until it begins to snap, crackle and pop. Gradually pour in the broth and bring to a boil. Reduce heat to medium-low and cook covered for 15 to 20 minutes, or until the grains are tender but still chewy and most of the broth has been absorbed. (This may take up to 30 minutes.) Fluff with a fork, remove from heat and let stand covered for 5 to 10 minutes.

3. **TO SERVE:** Stir in the parsley and serve immediately.

Makes 4 cups (1 L) · One serving = 1 cup (250 mL)

2 tsp (10 mL)	canola oil
6 oz (175 g)	shiitake mushrooms, stems removed, caps thinly sliced (see sidebar)
3	shallots, chopped
1 tsp (5 mL)	dried thyme leaves
¼ tsp (1 mL)	freshly ground black pepper
1 cup (250 mL)	red quinoa, rinsed and drained
1¾ cups (435 mL)	vegetable broth
¼ cup (60 mL)	chopped flat-leaf parsley

Look for thick domed shiitake caps that curl under and have pale spots or a light bloom. Wipe clean or lightly rinse before using. Always cut off the tough stems and either reserve for stock or toss into the composter.

Nutrition per serving

248 calories	6 g total fat	0 g saturated fat
0 mg cholesterol	214 mg sodium	43 g carbohydrates
6 g fibre	9 g sugars	8 g protein

Excellent source of iron.

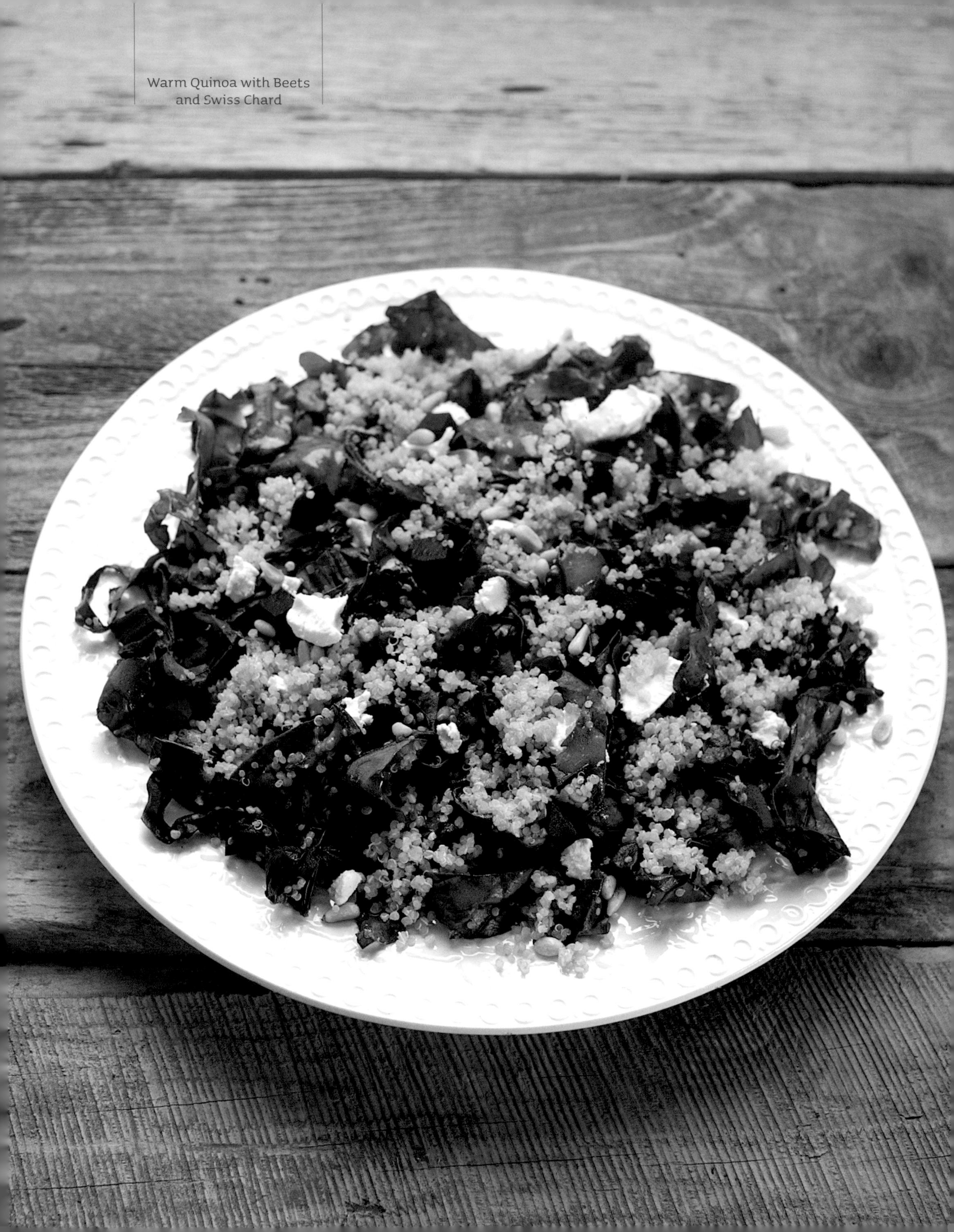

Warm Quinoa with Beets and Swiss Chard

This gorgeous dish is wonderful for an everyday side and will add a huge splash of colour and flavour to a buffet table.

YEAR ROUND

Joan Ttooulias, PHEc

Warm Quinoa with Beets and Swiss Chard

1. Preheat the oven to 375°F (190°C). Wrap the beets loosely in foil. Roast for 40 to 45 minutes, or until the beets are tender when pierced with the tip of a sharp knife.

2. Once the beets are cooked, place the quinoa in a large saucepan, add the broth and bring to a boil. Reduce heat to medium-low and cook covered for 15 to 20 minutes. The quinoa is done when the grains are translucent and all the liquid has been absorbed. Fluff with a fork, remove from heat and let stand covered for 5 to 10 minutes.

3. When the beets are cool enough to handle, peel and dice. Set aside.

4. DRESSING: In a large bowl, whisk together the oil, balsamic and red wine vinegars and the Dijon mustard.

5. In a large frying pan over medium heat, heat the oil. Add the garlic and Swiss chard and sauté for 2 to 4 minutes, just until the Swiss chard wilts.

6. Remove from heat and add to the large bowl with the dressing. Toss to coat.

7. Add the cooked quinoa and beets, tossing mixture gently to coat all the ingredients.

8. TO SERVE: Sprinkle the crumbled goat cheese on top, garnish with pine nuts (if using) and serve immediately.

Makes 8 cups (2 L) • One serving = 1 cup (250 mL)

3	medium beets (about 12 oz/375 g), scrubbed well and trimmed
1 cup (250 mL)	quinoa, rinsed and drained
1½ cups (375 mL)	vegetable broth
1 Tbsp (15 mL)	extra virgin olive oil
2	cloves garlic, finely chopped
1	bunch Swiss chard, washed, stems removed and finely chopped
1 cup (250 mL)	crumbled goat cheese

DRESSING

2 Tbsp (30 mL)	extra virgin olive oil
2 Tbsp (30 mL)	balsamic vinegar
1 Tbsp (15 mL)	red wine vinegar
1 Tbsp (15 mL)	Dijon or grainy mustard
¼ cup (60 mL)	toasted pine nuts for garnish (optional)

Nutrition per serving

200 calories	11 g total fat	4 g saturated fat
9 mg cholesterol	355 mg sodium	20 g carbohydrates
3 g fibre	3 g sugars	7 g protein

Excellent source of magnesium.

Pepitas or hulled green pumpkin seeds take this easy-to-make pilaf to another taste level. NOTE: You can find pepitas in larger grocery stores with the nuts and seeds. Mushroom bouillon cubes are available in some larger grocery stores and at most Italian grocers.

Pepitas Pilaf

1½ cups (375 mL)	water
1	mushroom bouillon cube
1 cup (250 mL)	quinoa, rinsed and drained
¼ cup (60 mL)	pepitas
½ cup (125 mL)	chopped cilantro
2	green onions, thinly sliced
1 tsp (5 mL)	red pepper flakes, or to taste (see sidebar)
½ tsp (2 mL)	freshly ground black pepper
½ tsp (2 mL)	ground cumin
1	red pepper, seeded and finely chopped
Juice of ½	lime (about 1½ Tbsp/22 mL)
	Cilantro sprigs for garnish

Feel free to use 1 jalapeño pepper instead of the red pepper flakes for more heat in this dish. When using jalapeño peppers, wear gloves and avoid touching your face and eyes.

1. In a large saucepan, bring the water and bouillon cube to a boil.

2. Add the quinoa. Stir and return to a boil. Reduce heat to medium-low and cook covered for 15 to 20 minutes. The quinoa is done when the grains are translucent and all the liquid has been absorbed. Fluff with a fork, remove from heat and let stand covered for 5 to 10 minutes.

3. Meanwhile, toast the pepitas. Heat a medium frying pan over medium heat. No need to add any fat, since the seeds have enough in them to prevent sticking. Add the pepitas and gently toast, stirring occasionally, until they start to smell like—what else?—toasted pumpkin seeds. This takes about 5 minutes.

4. Remove lid from the quinoa pot and gently stir in the toasted seeds, cilantro, green onions, red pepper flakes, pepper, cumin, red pepper and lime juice.

5. **TO SERVE:** Garnish with a sprig of cilantro.

Makes 3 cups (750 mL) • One serving = ½ cup (125 mL)

Nutrition per serving

155 calories	5 g total fat	1 g saturated fat
0 mg cholesterol	125 mg sodium	24 g carbohydrates
3 g fibre	2 g sugars	6 g protein

Excellent source of vitamin C, magnesium and iron.

Goat feta has a tangy flavour and is the perfect addition to this side, balancing the flavours from the sweet potato.

Linda Lichtenberger, PHEc

Quinoa with Feta and Sweet Potato

1. Place the quinoa in a small saucepan, add the broth and bring to a boil. Reduce heat to medium-low and cook covered for 15 to 20 minutes. The quinoa is done when the grains are translucent and all the liquid has been absorbed. Fluff with a fork, remove from heat and let stand covered for 5 to 10 minutes.

2. Place the cubed sweet potatoes in a steamer basket. Place in a medium saucepan. Add 2 in (5 cm) of water to the saucepan. Cover and bring to a boil. Reduce to a medium heat and steam until tender, about 6 to 8 minutes.

3. Toss the feta cubes and green onions in a large bowl. Add the parsley and cranberries (if using).

4. **TO SERVE:** Toss in the cooked quinoa and sweet potatoes and serve immediately. This side goes well with grilled tofu.

Makes 4 cups (1 L) • One serving = ½ cup (125 mL)

½ cup (125 mL)	red quinoa, rinsed and drained
1 cup (250 mL)	vegetable broth
2 cups (500 mL)	cubed sweet potato, peeled and cut into ½-inch (1 cm) cubes
1 cup (250 mL)	goat feta, cut into ½-inch (1 cm) cubes
6	green onions, thinly sliced
¼ cup (60 mL)	chopped fresh parsley
1 Tbsp	dried cranberries (optional)

Nutrition per serving

127 calories	5 g total fat	3 g saturated fat
17 mg cholesterol	289 mg sodium	16 g carbohydrates
2 g fibre	4 g sugars	5 g protein

Excellent source of vitamin A.

FALL and WINTER

Olga Kaminskyj, PHEc

These little canoes can be served as a light lunch or as a side dish for family dinners but are elegant enough to serve at a dinner party.

Zucchini Canoes

4	medium to large zucchini
1 Tbsp (15 mL)	canola oil
1	small onion, minced
¼ cup (60 mL)	peeled grated carrot
1 can (19 oz/540 mL)	diced tomatoes, divided
½ cup (125 mL)	quinoa, rinsed and drained
2 cups (500 mL)	packed coarsely chopped fresh baby spinach
¼ cup (60 mL)	chopped toasted pecans (toasting optional)
¾ cup (185 mL)	grated extra-old cheddar cheese
1 Tbsp (15 mL)	chopped fresh parsley for garnish

1. Preheat the oven to 400°F (200°C). Line a 9- × 13-inch (23 × 33 cm) baking sheet with foil, curling up the ends so the tomato topping doesn't spill onto the sheet.

2. Cut each zucchini in half lengthwise. (Don't cut off the ends— you're going to make a canoe.) Using a teaspoon (preferably a dainty one like the kind your grandma may have had), scoop out the pulp to make 8 zucchini canoes. Make sure you don't end up going right through the peel. Set aside the pulp for another use (such as zucchini bread) or compost. Place the zucchini into the prepared pan cut sides up and close together.

3. In a large frying pan over medium heat, heat the oil. Add the onion and carrots and sauté for 3 minutes.

4. Set aside 1 cup (250 mL) of the canned tomatoes. Add the remaining tomatoes to the pan and bring to a boil.

5. Stir in the quinoa. Cover pan and reduce heat to medium-low. Simmer for 12 minutes, or until the quinoa is tender. Stir in the spinach and pecans. Cover and simmer for 2 minutes, or until the spinach has wilted.

6. Mound up the quinoa mixture into the zucchini canoes. Spoon the reserved tomatoes over top. Sprinkle with the cheese.

7. Bake for 16 to 18 minutes, or until the zucchini are tender and the cheese has melted. Sprinkle with parsley.

Makes 8 zucchini canoes • One serving = 1 zucchini canoe

Nutrition per serving

159 calories	9 g total fat	3 g saturated fat
11 mg cholesterol	286 mg sodium	15 g carbohydrates
3 g fibre	4 g sugars	7 g protein

FALL and **WINTER**

Rosemarie Superville,
PHEc

Who says you can't make risotto out of quinoa? This creamy risotto will make a believer out of you. NOTE: To add a flavour twist, use a mixture of wild mushrooms. And for a main dish risotto to try, see page 130.

Mushroom Risotto

1 cup (250 mL)	quinoa, rinsed and drained
2¼ cups (560 mL)	vegetable broth, divided
1 Tbsp (15 mL)	extra virgin olive oil
1	onion, diced
8 oz (235 g)	white or cremini mushrooms, thinly sliced
3	cloves garlic, minced
2 tsp (10 mL)	chopped fresh thyme
1 Tbsp (15 mL)	whole wheat flour
1 Tbsp (15 mL)	balsamic vinegar
¼ cup (60 mL)	freshly grated Parmesan Reggiano cheese
	Freshly ground black pepper to taste

1. Place the quinoa in a large saucepan, add 2 cups (500 mL) of the broth and bring to a boil. Reduce heat to medium-low and cook covered for 10 to 15 minutes. The quinoa is done when the grains are translucent and most of the liquid has been absorbed.

2. Meanwhile, in a large non-stick frying pan, heat the oil over medium heat. Add the onion and sauté for about 2 minutes, or until the onion has softened.

3. Add the mushrooms and cook, stirring occasionally, for about 5 minutes, or until browned and juicy.

4. Add the garlic, thyme and flour. Cook, stirring, for another minute.

5. Stir in the cooked quinoa, balsamic vinegar and enough reserved broth to make the mixture creamy. (If you want it really creamy, add all of the reserved ¼ cup/60 mL of broth.)

6. **TO SERVE:** Stir in the grated cheese. Season with ground pepper and voila!—quinoa risotto.

Makes about 4 cups (1 L) • One serving = 1 cup (250 mL)

Nutrition per serving

274 calories	8 g total fat	2 g saturated fat
5 mg cholesterol	369 mg sodium	41 g carbohydrates
5 g fibre	5 g sugars	11 g protein

Excellent source of magnesium, iron and zinc.

Here's a different spin on spring rolls, using black beans as part of the filling. This recipe uses rice paper sheets that have been dipped in a "saffron tea" to give them a golden hue. Serve as an appetizer or as a side dish.

YEAR ROUND

Joan Ttooulias, PHEc

Vegan Spring Rolls

1. **SAFFRON TEA:** In a small saucepan, heat the water to boiling point. Add the saffron. Remove from heat and let steep covered for 15 minutes.

2. **DRESSING:** Meanwhile, in a small bowl, whisk together the toasted sesame seeds, vinegar, soy sauce and oil. Reserve ½ cup (125 mL)—this becomes the dipping sauce. Store in the fridge.

3. **FILLING:** In a large bowl, combine the cooked quinoa, green onions, red and orange peppers, beans, jalapeño, ginger and garlic. Add the rest of the dressing and toss.

4. Remove the saffron from the saffron tea and discard the threads. Pour the tea into a large, wide, shallow round container or frying pan. Soak one rice paper sheet in the saffron tea for 20 to 30 seconds, or until softened. Gently shake off excess tea.

5. **TO ASSEMBLE:** Spoon ¼ cup (60 mL) of the filling in a line in the centre of the rice paper. Fold in both sides of rice paper and roll from the bottom until sealed. Continue to soak and fill the rice papers. Store the assembled rolls in a dish lined and covered with moist paper towel or a tea towel.

6. **TO SERVE:** Serve as soon as all of the rolls have been assembled. If desired, place the rolls on finely chopped spinach. Pour the reserved dressing into a small bowl to serve alongside as dipping sauce.

Makes 18 rolls • One serving = 1 roll

SAFFRON TEA

½ cup (125 mL)	water
Pinch	saffron threads, crushed between fingers
18 6-inch (15 cm)	rice paper sheets

DRESSING & DIPPING SAUCE

¼ cup (60 mL)	toasted sesame seeds, black or white (see sidebar)
¼ cup (60 mL)	seasoned rice vinegar
3 Tbsp + 1 tsp (50 mL)	lower-sodium soy sauce
2 Tbsp (30 mL)	sesame seed oil

FILLING

1 cup (250 mL)	cooked quinoa made with water (see pages 5–6)
2	green onions, thinly sliced lengthwise
½	red pepper, diced
½	orange pepper, diced
1 can (19 oz/540 mL)	black beans, well rinsed and drained
1	jalapeño pepper, deseeded and diced (see sidebar page 94)
1 Tbsp + 2 tsp (25 mL)	grated ginger
1 Tbsp + 2 tsp (25 mL)	minced garlic
	Finely chopped spinach for serving plate (optional)

To toast sesame seeds, place them in a small non-stick frying pan. Toast over medium heat, until golden brown, stirring often to prevent burning.

Nutrition per serving

93 calories	2 g total fat	0 g saturated fat
0 mg cholesterol	97 mg sodium	15 g carbohydrates
2 g fibre	1 g sugars	4 g protein

Curry paste from a jar not only simplifies this healthy vegetarian dish, but also adds an authentic curry flavour. Using whole cardamom pods rather than ground cardamom punches up the flavours even more. NOTE: You can find green cardamom pods in a bulk food store or in the spice aisle of your grocery store.

Curried Quinoa, Sweet Potato and Cauliflower

8	whole green cardamom pods
1	onion, chopped
2 Tbsp (30 mL)	Indian curry paste (mild or hot)
1 large or 2 small	sweet potatoes (1 lb/500 g), peeled and cut into ½-inch (1 cm) pieces
½ cup (125 mL)	quinoa, rinsed and drained
1½ cups (375 mL)	vegetable broth
3 cups (750 mL)	cauliflower florets
1 cup (250 mL)	frozen peas, no need to thaw

1. Smash the cardamom pods with the side of a heavy knife. Remove brown seeds, set aside and discard all of the pods.

2. Place a large, heavy saucepan over low heat. Add the onion and curry paste, stirring in the paste thoroughly. Cook, stirring constantly, for 1 minute.

3. Stir in the sweet potato and cardamom seeds. Cook for 2 to 3 minutes.

4. Stir in the quinoa and broth. Cover and bring to a boil over high heat. Reduce heat to low and simmer covered for 10 minutes.

5. Add the cauliflower and bring to a boil. Reduce heat and simmer covered until the vegetables are tender, about 15 to 20 minutes. Stir in the peas and heat through.

6. **TO SERVE:** This dish goes really well with whole wheat naan. Warm the naan in a toaster oven or cut into four pieces and toast in a regular toaster. Or try the recipe for Spinach Roti on page 86.

Makes 6 cups (1.5 L) • One serving = 1½ cups (375 mL)

Nutrition per serving

236 calories	5 g total fat	0 g saturated fat
0 mg cholesterol	256 mg sodium	41 g carbohydrates
7 g fibre	11 g sugars	7 g protein

Excellent source of vitamins A and C.

CHAPTER SIX

Main Dishes

Main Dishes

VEGETARIANS NEED TO MAKE SURE that the main course, or their chief meal of the day, supplies enough protein to maintain good health. Protein helps your body build and repair all systems, helps to form enzymes and hormones and is needed to help build antibodies to fight off infections.

Although quinoa is a complete protein (it contains all essential building blocks of protein, called amino acids), it *doesn't contain high levels* of protein. The average adult needs approximately 50 to 175 grams of protein per day to maintain health. The range reflects body weight and activity levels based on a 2,000 kcal diet. This chart shows how quinoa compares to other single servings of protein-rich foods.

FOOD TYPE	SERVING SIZE	PROTEIN PROVIDED
Cooked quinoa	½ cup/125 mL	3 g
Walnut halves	¼ cup/60 mL	4 g
Almonds	¼ cup/60 mL	8 g
Peanuts	¼ cup/60 mL	10 g
Skim milk	1 cup/250 mL	9 g
Any dried cooked beans	¾ cup/185 mL	11 g
Eggs	2 large	12 g
Firm tofu	¾ cup/185 mL	20 g

As this chart illustrates, even though the 3 grams of protein in quinoa is a complete protein, you'd have to eat a lot of quinoa to make your required 50 to 175 grams for the day. Pairing quinoa with other vegetarian protein sources such as beans, nuts, milk products, eggs or tofu helps vegetarians reach the levels of protein needed to maintain health.

The recipes in this section range from 9 to 22 grams of protein per serving. When choosing a lower-protein dish, make sure to serve it with a glass of either milk or an organic soy beverage to help increase the level of protein consumed at that meal.

For super protein-rich dishes, try the tasty Goat Cheese, Red Pepper and Arugula Quiche (page 142) or the spin on the classic sloppy joes (page 113), both weighing in with 16 grams of protein per serving. The Slow Cooker Vegetarian Lasagna (page 128) hits a home run with 22 grams of protein per serving and a whole lot of fabulous flavours. As long as you have eggs in your fridge, dinner can be ready in a jiffy. Add the goodness of quinoa and any egg dish hits a new level of healthy. Try one of the six egg dishes for a quick, easy, delicious dinner option.

Altogether, this section offers over 30 delicious and nutritious recipes to try, one for each day of the month! Have fun deciding which one to sample first.

Mediterranean Flavours

Omelettes and Other Egg Dishes

This great family-friendly casserole is a variation on a traditional shepherd's pie. Serve with a tossed green salad and you are in the zone—the healthy zone!

Mexi Meatless Shepherd's Pie

2 lb (1 kg)	sweet potatoes, scrubbed well and pierced all over with a fork
1 Tbsp (15 mL)	canola oil
1	onion, chopped
1	red pepper, diced
2	cloves garlic, minced
2 tsp (10 mL)	ground cumin
1 can (19 oz/540 mL)	black beans, no salt added, well rinsed and drained
1 cup (250 mL)	cooked quinoa made with water (see pages 5–6)
1 cup (250 mL)	frozen corn, no need to thaw
1 cup (250 mL)	mild or medium salsa, deli-style
¼ cup (60 mL)	light sour cream
¼ cup (60 mL)	finely chopped cilantro
¼ tsp (1 mL)	freshly ground black pepper (optional)
¼ cup (60 mL)	thinly sliced green onion or chopped cilantro for garnish

1. Preheat the oven to 350°F (175°C). Bake the sweet potatoes for 60 minutes, or until tender. Alternatively, microwave at High for 8 to 12 minutes. Cool until easy to handle.

2. Lightly grease an 8-cup (2 L) baking dish with canola oil or line with wet parchment paper (see page 10). Set aside.

3. In a large soup pot or Dutch oven, heat the oil over medium heat. Add the onion, red pepper, garlic and cumin. Cook, stirring often, for 5 to 7 minutes. Stir in the black beans, cooked quinoa, corn and salsa until well combined. Remove from heat.

4. Pour into the prepared pan. If you used a microwave to cook the sweet potatoes, at this point preheat the oven to 350°F (175°C).

5. Meanwhile, cut the cooled sweet potatoes in half and scrape out the flesh. Discard the skins. Mash the sweet potato well with the sour cream. Stir in the cilantro. Season with pepper if desired.

6. For a rustic look (as in the photo), spoon the sweet potato mixture over the quinoa mixture in heaping teaspoonfuls. (If you like more conformity, spoon on and spread out.)

7. Bake for 30 minutes, or until heated through and bubbly. Sprinkle top of the casserole with green onion or cilantro (if using) to garnish.

Makes 6 cups (1.5 L) • One serving = 1½ cups (375 mL)

Nutrition per serving (1½ cups/375 mL)

413 calories	6 g total fat	1 g saturated fat
2 mg cholesterol	544 mg sodium	75 g carbohydrates
13 g fibre	24 g sugars	13 g protein

Excellent source of vitamins A and C.

FALL and **WINTER**

Jennifer MacKenzie,
PHEc

Wild rice and quinoa are natural partners in this patty. Don't skip adding the mango chutney and yogurt; they really meld the flavours together. NOTE: The whole wheat flour helps the cakes stick together, but if you want to keep these gluten free, use the quinoa flour. The cakes will be a little more fragile when shaping and cooking.

Curried Quinoa and Wild Rice Cakes

3¾ cups (935 mL)	water
⅓ cup (80 mL)	wild rice, rinsed and drained
Pinch	salt
¾ cup (185 mL)	quinoa, rinsed and drained
1 tsp (5 mL)	extra virgin olive oil
2	green onions, finely chopped
2	cloves garlic, minced
½ cup (125 mL)	finely diced red pepper
2 Tbsp (30 mL)	curry paste (mild, medium or hot, to taste)
¼ cup (60 mL)	whole wheat or quinoa flour (see page 7)
1	omega-3 egg, beaten
1 Tbsp (15 mL)	canola oil, divided
½ cup (125 mL)	plain low-fat yogurt
2 Tbsp + 2 tsp (40 mL)	mango chutney

1. In a large saucepan, bring the water to a boil over high heat. Add the wild rice and salt. Reduce heat and boil gently for 30 minutes. Stir in the quinoa, then reduce heat to medium-low and simmer covered for 15 to 20 minutes, or until wild rice kernels begin to burst open, quinoa is translucent and tender, and most of the liquid has been absorbed. Fluff with a fork, remove from heat and let stand covered for 5 minutes. Drain away any excess water and spread out in a large baking dish and let cool to room temperature.

2. Meanwhile, in a large non-stick frying pan, heat the oil over medium heat. Add the green onions, garlic, red pepper and curry paste and sauté for about 3 minutes, or until softened. Let cool slightly. Transfer to a bowl and wipe out the pan.

3. Place about 1 cup (250 mL) of the quinoa mixture in a large bowl and mash with a potato masher until slightly pasty. Add the remaining quinoa mixture and sautéed vegetables. Sprinkle with the flour and stir in the egg with a fork until evenly blended.

4. Reheat the frying pan over medium heat. Add ½ Tbsp (7 mL) of the canola oil. Scoop portions of about ⅓ cup (80 mL) of the mixture and place into the hot pan. Gently press down with the bottom of the measuring cup to make a patty. You should be able to make eight patties in total, frying four at a time.

5. Fry about 3 to 4 minutes per side, until browned on both sides and hot in the centre. Repeat with the remaining four patties, using the rest of the oil.

6. **TO SERVE:** Top each patty with 1 Tbsp (15 mL) of yogurt and 1 tsp (5 mL) of chutney. Serve these with a mixed green salad. The patties can be made ahead, cooked, cooled and refrigerated for up to 1 day. Reheat them in a 375°F (190°C) oven for about 15 minutes before serving.

Makes 8 cakes • One serving = 2 cakes

Nutrition per serving

339 calories	12 g total fat	1 g saturated fat
48 mg cholesterol	48 mg sodium	49 g carbohydrates
5 g fibre	6 g sugars	11 g protein

Excellent source of vitamin C and iron.

YEAR ROUND

Steve Dubé,
SHEA student member

Finding a tasty quinoa protein-rich burger recipe is like searching for a needle in a haystack. Well, you need search no more—we've found it for you.

Weekend Burgers

1–2 slices	100% whole-grain whole wheat bread
¾ cup (185 mL)	cooked quinoa made with vegetable broth (see pages 5–6)
1 can (19 oz/540 mL)	kidney beans, well rinsed and drained
¼ cup (60 mL)	silken tofu (see sidebar)
½ cup (125 mL)	diced carrots
2	green onions, thinly sliced
1 Tbsp (15 mL)	ground cumin
¼ tsp (1 mL)	freshly ground pepper, or to taste
1 Tbsp (15 mL)	canola oil
4	100% whole wheat buns or pitas

You can find silken tofu in either the produce section or in a Tetra Pak in the Asian food section of large grocery stores. Use any leftover silken tofu in a blender drink.

1. Pulse the bread in a food processor to make 1 cup (250 mL) of fresh breadcrumbs. Place in a large bowl.

2. Add the cooked quinoa, beans and tofu. Mash with a potato masher until well blended.

3. Add the carrots, green onions, cumin and pepper. Stir to combine (mixture should still be slightly chunky).

4. Form the mixture into four ¾-inch-thick (2 cm) patties. If too soft, refrigerate for 15 minutes to firm up. **TIP:** Use an ice cream scoop or a measuring cup if desired to make the patties.

5. In a large non-stick frying pan, heat the oil over medium heat. Cook the burgers until browned and cooked through, about 8 to 10 minutes per side. The longer you cook without burning, the crunchier the outside becomes.

6. **TO SERVE:** Meanwhile, toast the buns or warm the pitas in the oven and spread with your favourite toppings (try hummus, salad greens, jarred roasted red bell peppers, tzatziki sauce, avocado or your favourite salsa). Top each with a cooked patty and serve immediately.

Makes 4 large patties • One serving = 1 patty (without bun or topping)

Nutrition per serving

397 calories	9 g total fat	1 g saturated fat
0 mg cholesterol	603 mg sodium	62 g carbohydrates
10 g fibre	6 g sugars	17 g protein

Excellent source of folate, magnesium and iron.

Serve these along with some steamed broccoli for a yummy and nutritious dinner.

YEAR ROUND

Cindy Fendall, PHEc

Baked Patties with Cilantro Yogurt

1. **CILANTRO YOGURT:** In a medium bowl, combine all the ingredients. This can be made up to 24 hours ahead of time and refrigerated, covered, until serving time.

2. **PATTIES:** Place the quinoa in a large saucepan, add the broth and bring to a boil. Reduce heat to medium-low and cook covered for 15 to 20 minutes. The quinoa is done when the grains are translucent and all the liquid has been absorbed. Fluff with a fork, remove from heat and let stand covered for 5 to 10 minutes.

3. Preheat the oven to 425°F (220°C). Line a large rimmed baking sheet (15- × 11-inch/38 × 28 cm) with parchment paper.

4. In a large non-stick frying pan, heat the oil over medium heat. Add the onion and carrots. Sauté about 5 minutes, until the onion has softened.

5. Add the kale, flaxseed, garlic, paprika, cayenne pepper, pepper and lemon juice and cook for another minute. Remove from heat and set aside until cool to the touch.

6. Combine the cooked quinoa, yogurt, egg and onion/kale mixture in a large bowl. Shape the mixture into ½ cup (125 mL) patties and place on the prepared baking sheet. Gently press down until the patties are about ½ inch (1 cm) thick.

7. Bake for 15 minutes, until golden brown. While the patties are baking, if you have not already done so, prepare the cilantro yogurt.

8. **TO SERVE:** Serve with cilantro yogurt and a slice of avocado.

Makes 8 patties • One serving = 2 patties with ¼ cup (60 mL) cilantro yogurt

Nutrition per serving

416 calories	19 g total fat	3 g saturated fat
53 mg cholesterol	120 mg sodium	50 g carbohydrates
10 g fibre	9 g sugars	15 g protein

Excellent source of vitamin A, riboflavin, folate, vitamin B12, vitamin C, magnesium, iron and zinc.

CILANTRO YOGURT

1 cup (250 mL)	plain non-fat yogurt
¼ cup (60 mL)	finely chopped cilantro
1 tsp (5 mL)	lemon zest
2 Tbsp (30 mL)	fresh lemon juice
1	clove garlic, finely chopped

PATTIES

1 cup (250 mL)	quinoa, rinsed and drained
1¾ cups (435 mL)	water
1 Tbsp (15 mL)	canola oil
¼ cup (60 mL)	finely chopped onion
1 cup (250 mL)	grated carrots, scrubbed well, peel left on
1 cup (250 mL)	coarsely chopped kale, stem removed
¼ cup (60 mL)	ground flaxseed
1	clove garlic, finely chopped
½ tsp (2 mL)	paprika
⅛ tsp (0.5 mL)	cayenne pepper
½ tsp (2 mL)	freshly ground black pepper
1 Tbsp (15 mL)	fresh lemon juice
½ cup (125 mL)	plain non-fat yogurt
1	omega-3 egg
	Avocado (optional)

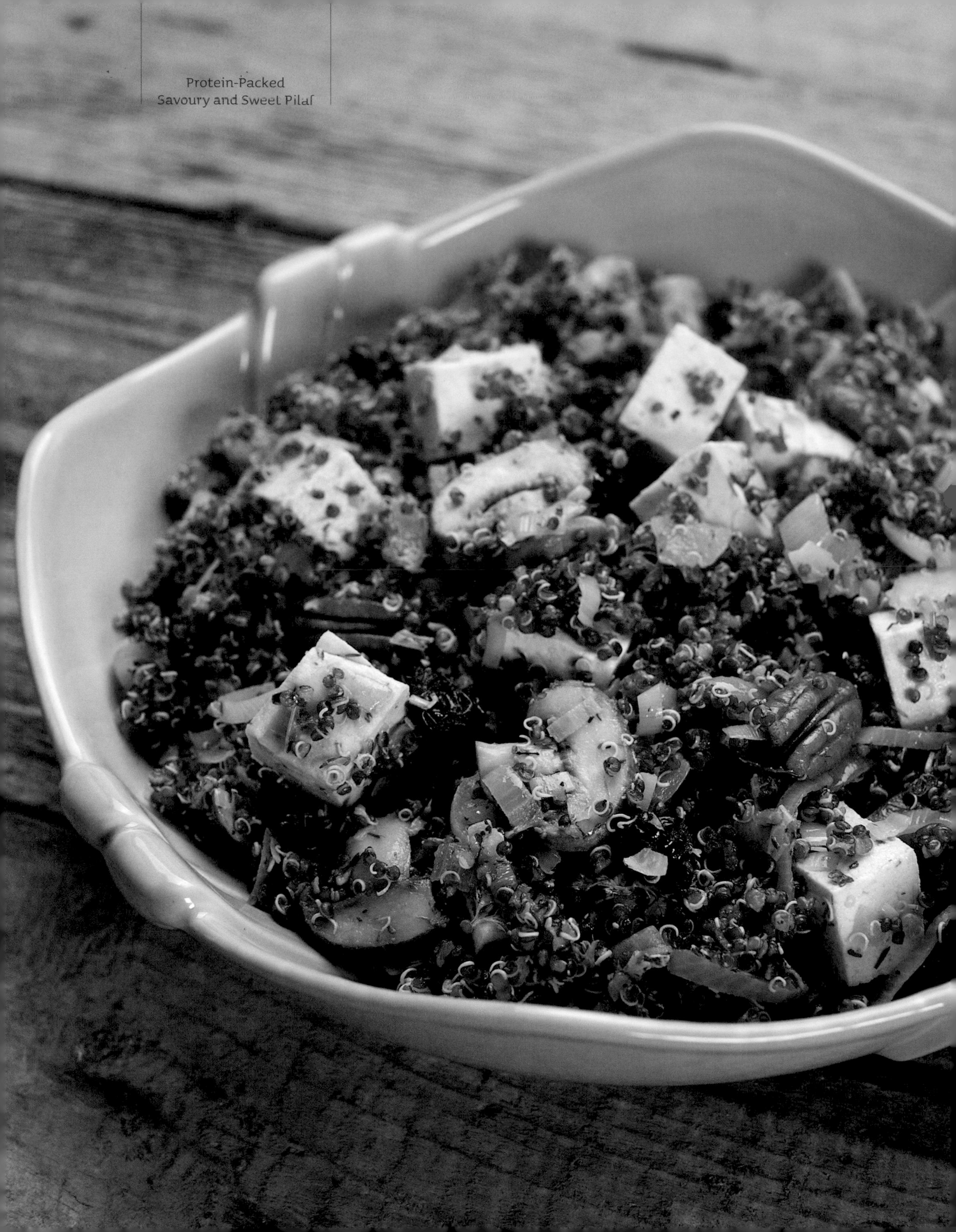

Protein-Packed
Savoury and Sweet Pilaf

This protein-rich dish stands out in the nutrient *and* the flavour department. The sage and thyme combined with the sweetness from the dried cranberries give this dish its fabulous fall flavours. NOTE: Add 1 cup (250 mL) of pomegranate seeds to add more festive flavours, some crunch and a big hit of antioxidants. See page 9 on how to seed a pomegranate. BONUS: The pilaf can be prepared the day ahead, making it great for a holiday buffet.

stoppe here

FALL and **WINTER**

Jan Main, PHEc

Protein-Packed Savoury and Sweet Pilaf

1. Place the quinoa in a large saucepan, add the water and bring to a boil. Reduce heat to medium-low and cook covered for 15 to 18 minutes. The quinoa is done when the grains are translucent and all the water has been absorbed. Fluff with a fork, remove from heat and let stand covered for 5 to 10 minutes. Remove lid and let quinoa cool while the vegetables are cooking.

2. Meanwhile, heat a separate medium saucepan over medium heat. Add the oil, leeks, onion, mushrooms, garlic, tofu, thyme and sage. Stir well. Cook covered for 5 to 10 minutes, stirring occasionally, until the vegetables are wilted.

3. Stir the hot vegetable mixture into the cooled quinoa together with the pecans, dried cranberries and pepper.

4. **TO SERVE:** Sprinkle the quinoa mixture with the parsley and gently fold in. Serve immediately. Alternatively, cover and refrigerate overnight. To reheat, sprinkle with ½ cup (125 mL) warm water and heat in a 350°F (175°C) oven about 25 to 30 minutes or microwave until warm.

Makes 8 cups (2 L) • One serving = 2 cups (500 mL)

1 cup (250 mL)	red quinoa, rinsed and drained
2 cups (500 mL)	vegetable broth
2 Tbsp (30 mL)	canola oil
1	leek, cleaned, trimmed, white part only, sliced into thin coins (see page 8)
1	onion, chopped
4 oz (120 g)	white or cremini mushrooms, cleaned and sliced
1	clove garlic, crushed
⅔ lb (350 g)	extra-firm tofu, cut into ½-inch (1 cm) cubes
2 tsp (10 mL)	dried thyme leaves
1 tsp (5 mL)	ground sage
⅓ cup (80 mL)	toasted pecan halves (toasting optional)
½ cup (125 mL)	dried cranberries
¼ tsp (1 mL)	freshly ground black pepper
¼ cup (60 mL)	finely chopped fresh parsley

To wash or not to wash mushrooms: that is the question. Mushrooms Canada recommends a quick rinse in a strainer followed by *patting dry* with paper towels or a clean tea towel.

Nutrition per serving

482 calories	21 g total fat	2 g saturated fat
0 mg cholesterol	248 mg sodium	57 g carbohydrates
8 g fibre	16 g sugars	18 g protein

Excellent source of folate, magnesium, iron and zinc.

FALL and **WINTER**

Emily Richards, PHEc

These "meatballs" are easy to serve up with your favourite whole-grain pasta, brown rice or cooked quinoa dish, or you could put them in a sandwich for lunch the next day. Use your favourite homemade pasta sauce or pick up a sauce that lists tomatoes as the first ingredient. NOTE: You will need either a blender or a food processor to make the soft 100% whole-grain whole wheat breadcrumbs.

Eggplant "Meatballs"

1	eggplant (about 1¼ lb/625 g)
½ cup (125 mL)	quinoa, rinsed and drained
¾ cup (185 mL)	vegetable broth
4 cups (1 L)	soft whole wheat breadcrumbs (4–5 slices 100% whole-grain whole wheat bread)
1 Tbsp (15 mL)	Italian seasoning
1	omega-3 egg, beaten
⅓ cup (80 mL)	freshly grated Parmesan cheese
3 Tbsp (45 mL)	chopped fresh parsley
2	cloves garlic, minced
¼ tsp (1 mL)	red pepper flakes
1–2 Tbsp (15–30 mL)	extra virgin olive oil
2 cups (500 mL)	pasta or tomato sauce, warmed

1. Line two large baking sheets with parchment paper and set aside. Cut the eggplant into 2-inch (5 cm) chunks and place in a steamer basket in a medium saucepan. Add about ½ cup (125 mL) water. Cover and bring to a boil. Cook for about 15 to 20 minutes, or until the eggplant is very tender. Drain well and set aside to cool slightly.

2. Meanwhile, in a small saucepan, bring the quinoa and broth to a boil. Reduce heat to medium-low and cook covered for about 15 to 18 minutes, or until the quinoa is translucent and all the liquid has been absorbed. Set aside covered to cool slightly.

3. Preheat the oven to 400°F (200°C). Mix together the breadcrumbs and Italian seasoning. Remove 1½ cups (375 mL) and reserve. Place the remaining breadcrumbs onto a medium low-rimmed plate or baking dish. You will roll the meatballs in these crumbs.

4. Place the cooked eggplant in a large bowl and mash with a fork. Add the cooked quinoa, egg, reserved 1½ cups (375 mL) of breadcrumbs, cheese, parsley, garlic and red pepper flakes. Stir until well combined.

5. Using about 2 Tbsp (30 mL), make an oval-shaped "meatball" and lightly roll it in the breadcrumbs on the dish. Place the meatballs on one of the prepared baking sheets. Repeat with remaining mixture to make 15 meatballs in total.

6. In a large non-stick frying pan, heat the oil over medium-high heat and brown the meatballs for about 2 minutes per side, or until golden. Place them on the second prepared baking sheet (you need two baking sheets to avoid cross contamination because of the raw egg). Bake in the centre of the oven for about 10 minutes, or until they heat through.

7. Meanwhile, in a small saucepan over low heat, warm the tomato sauce.

8. **TO SERVE:** Serve meatballs with about ⅓ cup (80 mL) sauce per serving.

Makes 15 meatballs • One serving = 3 meatballs with ⅓ cup (80 mL) sauce

Nutrition per serving

322 calories	11 g total fat	3 g saturated fat
44 mg cholesterol	551 mg sodium	45 g carbohydrates
10 g fibre	10 g sugars	12 g protein

Excellent source of iron.

Mushrooms are the not-so-secret ingredient in this dinner idea. Perhaps more secret is the fact that mushrooms can help strengthen your immune system and contain vitamin D. NOTE: This recipe is a hit with kids of all ages, but for the *big kids in your family* (a.k.a. the adults) who want it spicy, feel free to add hot sauce.

YEAR ROUND

Anna Shier,
OHEA student member

"Sloppy Mushroom Joes"

1. Place the quinoa in a small saucepan, add the water and bring to a boil. Reduce heat to medium-low and cook covered for 15 to 20 minutes. The quinoa is done when the grains are translucent and all the water has been absorbed. Fluff with a fork, remove from heat and let stand covered for 5 to 10 minutes.

2. Heat a large non-stick frying pan over medium heat. Add the oil and onion and sauté for 4 to 5 minutes, or until soft.

3. Add the minced garlic and mushrooms and let sit to brown (see sidebar page 118). Let them brown, then sauté gently for about 3 to 5 minutes or until golden brown on both sides.

4. Add the green and red peppers, celery, chili powder, paprika, oregano and pepper and sauté for 3 to 4 minutes or until the peppers are tender.

5. Add the tomatoes, tomato paste, water, ketchup and black beans. Simmer uncovered until the mixture thickens, about 5 minutes.

6. Add the cooked quinoa and mix well. Spoon the mixture onto 100% whole-grain buns, top with some low-fat cheese, if desired, and add fixins. Serve with a mixed green salad for a complete stick-to-your-ribs meal. (If desired, toast buns.)

Makes 6 cups (1.5 L) sauce • One serving = 1 bun with ¾ cup (185 mL) sauce

½ cup (125 mL)	quinoa, rinsed and drained
1 cup (250 mL)	water
1 Tbsp (15 mL)	canola oil
1	onion, finely diced
3	cloves garlic, minced
8 cups (2 L)	diced portobello mushrooms (about 4–5)
1	green pepper, diced
1	red pepper, diced
1 cup (250 mL)	diced celery
1 Tbsp (15 mL)	chili powder
1 Tbsp (15 mL)	paprika
2 tsp (10 mL)	dried oregano leaves
½ tsp (2 mL)	freshly ground black pepper
1 can (14 oz/398 mL)	diced tomatoes
½ cup (125 mL)	tomato paste
¼ cup (60 mL)	water
1 Tbsp (15 mL)	low-sodium ketchup
1 can (19 oz/540 mL)	black beans, well rinsed and drained
8	100% whole-grain buns

Nutrition per serving

320 calories	6 g total fat	1 g saturated fat
0 mg cholesterol	354 mg sodium	56 g carbohydrates
11 g fibre	12 g sugars	16 g protein

Excellent source of thiamin, riboflavin, niacin, folate, vitamin C, magnesium, iron and zinc.

FALL and WINTER

Emily Richards, PHEc

This chili is easy to make for a weeknight meal and perfect when served with a mixed green salad. NOTE: Use your favourite canned bean as a substitute for the bean medley and look for no-salt-added options to reduce the sodium further if desired.

Quick Weeknight Chili

2 tsp (10 mL)	canola oil
3	shallots, chopped
3	cloves garlic, minced
1 Tbsp (15 mL)	chili powder
1 tsp (5 mL)	ground cumin
1 tsp (5 mL)	dried oregano leaves
1 cup (250 mL)	quinoa, rinsed and drained
1 can (28 oz/796 mL)	diced tomatoes
1 can (19 oz/540 mL)	mixed beans, well rinsed and drained
1½ cups (375 mL)	vegetable broth
1	green bell pepper, chopped
½ lb (250 g)	firm tofu
¼ cup (60 mL)	chopped fresh cilantro

1. In a large soup pot or Dutch oven, heat the oil over medium heat. Add the shallots and garlic and sauté until softened, about 3 minutes. Stir in the chili powder, cumin and oregano and sauté for another minute.

2. Add the quinoa and stir to coat with the herbs and spices. Pour in the tomatoes, beans, broth and green pepper. Finely crumble the tofu into the pot and stir to combine. Bring to a boil. Reduce heat to low and simmer covered for about 20 minutes, or until the quinoa is tender and the chili is thickened slightly.

3. **TO SERVE:** Stir in the cilantro just before serving. Serve with 100% whole grain bread if desired or unsalted 100% whole grain corn chips.

Makes 8 cups (2 L) · One serving = 1½ cups (375 mL)

Nutrition per serving

339 calories	9 g total fat	1 g saturated fat
0 mg cholesterol	564 mg sodium	48 g carbohydrates
10 g fibre	6 g sugars	19 g protein

Excellent source of vitamin C, magnesium and iron.

This smoky-flavoured chili recipe is made for a crowd, for the freezer or for both! For serving busy families, freeze the cooked chili in smaller containers and add the green onions and cilantro at serving time. For serving a crowd, place the green onions and cilantro in small bowls and let your guests serve themselves.

FALL and **WINTER**

Bridget Wilson, PHEc

Chipotle Chili

1. In a large soup pot or Dutch oven, heat the oil over medium heat. Add the onion and garlic and sauté for 5 minutes, or until softened.

2. Add the chili powder and cumin and stir for about 1 minute.

3. Add the tomatoes, kidney beans, black beans, red peppers, corn and chipotle pepper. Bring to a boil, then reduce heat to low and simmer covered for 15 minutes.

4. Stir in the quinoa. Reduce heat to medium-low and simmer covered for 25 minutes, or until the quinoa grains are tender.

5. **TO SERVE:** Stir in the green onions and cilantro just before serving. If desired, sprinkle with grated cheddar cheese. A little goes a long way.

Makes 12 cups (3 L) • One serving = 1½ cups (375 mL)

1 Tbsp (15 mL)	canola oil
1	onion, chopped
4	cloves garlic, minced
2 Tbsp (30 mL)	chili powder
1 Tbsp (15 mL)	ground cumin
2 cans (28 oz/796 mL)	diced tomatoes
1 can (19 oz/540 mL)	kidney beans, well rinsed and drained
1 can (19 oz/540 mL)	black beans, well rinsed and drained
2	medium red peppers, chopped
1 cup (250 mL)	frozen corn, no need to thaw
1 Tbsp (15 mL)	canned whole chipotle pepper, finely chopped (see sidebar)
1 cup (250 mL)	quinoa, rinsed and drained

TOPPINGS

½ cup (125 mL)	thinly sliced green onions (about 4)
½ cup (125 mL)	chopped cilantro
½ cup (125 mL)	grated cheddar cheese (optional)

Canned chipotle peppers can be found in the Mexican section of most grocery stores. Since this recipe calls for only 1 pepper, freeze the remainder in small resealable plastic storage bags for later use.

Nutrition per serving

283 calories	4 g total fat	0 g saturated fat
0 mg cholesterol	525 mg sodium	51 g carbohydrates
12 g fibre	10 g sugars	13 g protein

Excellent source of vitamin C and iron.

If you are having a crowd over for Grey Cup Sunday, this is the recipe for you. Make it in the afternoon and it will be ready by halftime.

Slow Cooker Three-Bean Chili

1 Tbsp (15 mL)	canola oil
1	onion, diced
3	cloves garlic, minced
8 oz (235 g)	white mushrooms, cut into quarters
1 can (28 oz/796 mL)	diced tomatoes
1 can (5½ oz/156 mL)	tomato paste
1 cup (250 mL)	vegetable broth
½ cup (125 mL)	quinoa, rinsed and drained
1 can (19 oz/540 mL)	black beans, well rinsed and drained
1 can (19 oz/540 mL)	red kidney beans, well rinsed and drained
1 can (19 oz/540 mL)	lentils, well rinsed and drained
1	red pepper, diced
1	green pepper, diced
½ cup (125 mL)	diced celery
1 cup (250 mL)	diced carrot
1	jalapeño pepper, seeded and finely diced (see sidebar page 94)
2 Tbsp (30 mL)	chili powder
2 Tbsp (30 mL)	dried basil leaves
1 Tbsp (15 mL)	dried oregano leaves
1 Tbsp (15 mL)	paprika
2 tsp (10 mL)	ground cumin
2 tsp (10 mL)	ground coriander
¼ tsp (1 mL)	cayenne pepper

1. Heat a large non-stick frying pan over medium heat. Add the oil and onion and sauté for 4 to 5 minutes, or until the onion has softened. Add the minced garlic and mushrooms and brown until most of the liquid evaporates (see sidebar page 118).

2. To a 6-quart (6 L) slow cooker, add the onion mixture, tomatoes, tomato paste, vegetable broth, quinoa, black beans, kidney beans and lentils. Mix until well blended.

3. Add both peppers, and the celery, carrot, jalapeño, chili powder, basil, oregano, paprika, cumin, coriander and cayenne pepper. Stir until well blended.

4. Set your slow cooker to High and cook for 4 to 4½ hours. Chili is done when the veggies are cooked through and soft.

5. **TO SERVE:** Simply stir and serve. Top with either grated cheddar cheese or low-fat sour cream or a little of both. If you have leftovers, try freezing lunch-sized portions for those days you want a quick lunch without the extra work.

Makes 16 cups (4 L) • One serving = 1½ cups (375 mL)

Nutrition per serving

203 calories	3 g total fat	0 g saturated fat
0 mg cholesterol	355 mg sodium	34 g carbohydrates
9 g fibre	5 g sugars	11 g protein

Excellent source of vitamin C and iron.

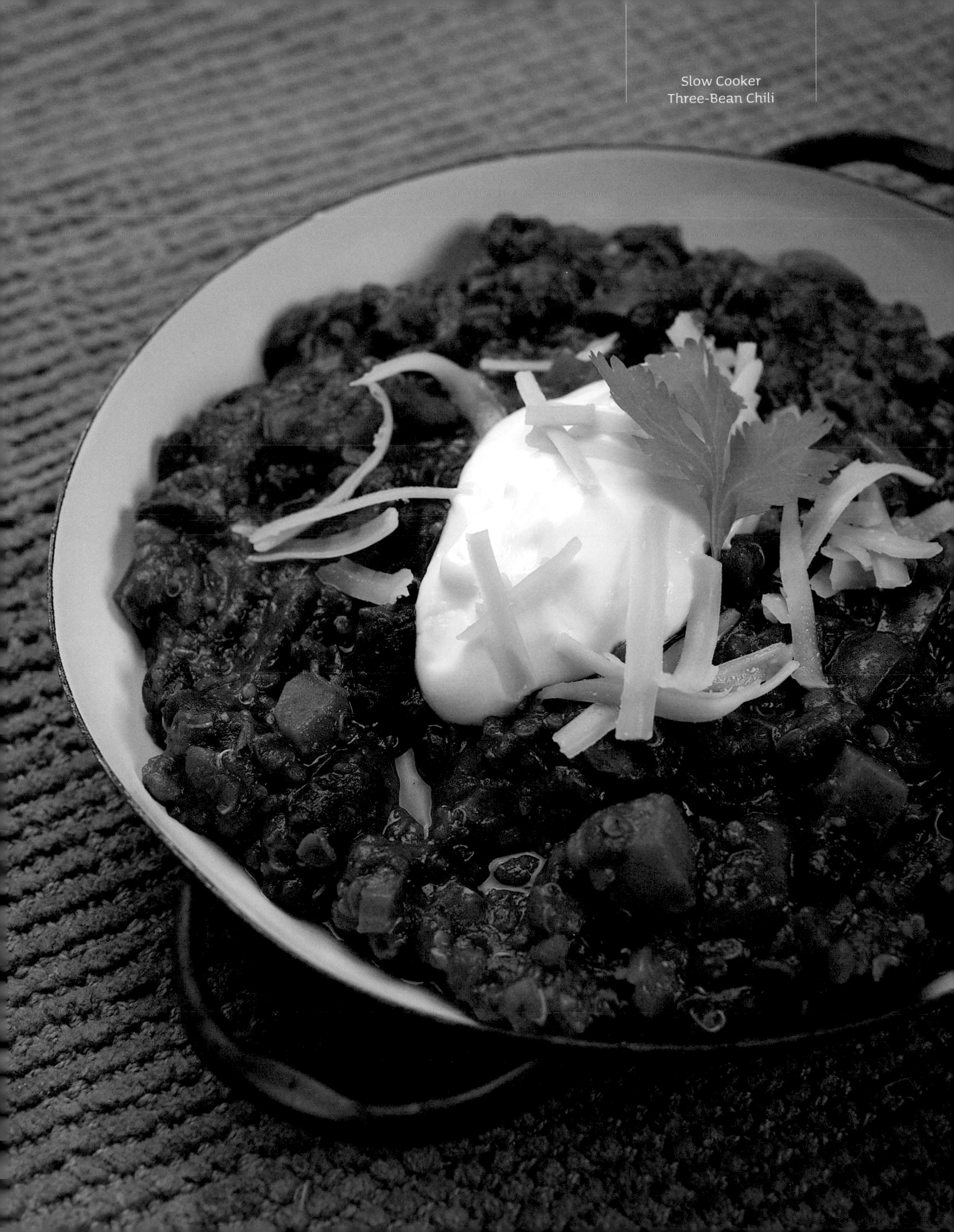

Slow Cooker
Three-Bean Chili

This colourful all-in-one dish is a great fall or winter supper to serve your family. Easy to make, this dinner can be on the table in about 30 minutes—quicker and way more nutritious than takeout. NOTE: If you can't find mini mushrooms, substitute 3 cups (750 mL) of thinly sliced white mushrooms.

Harvest Dinner

¼ cup (60 mL)	red quinoa, rinsed and drained
½ cup (125 mL)	water
1 Tbsp (30 mL)	canola oil
8 oz (235 g)	mini white mushrooms, thinly sliced
1	onion, diced
4	large cloves garlic, minced
2	medium carrots, scrubbed and diced
1 Tbsp (15 mL)	dried thyme leaves
1 tsp (5 mL)	dried rosemary
¼ tsp (1 mL)	freshly ground black pepper
½ cup (125 mL)	vegetable broth, divided
8 oz (235 g)	frozen shelled edamame no need to thaw (about 1¼ cups/310 mL) (see sidebar page 72)
4 oz (125 g) or	goat feta about ½ cup (125 mL)

When browning mushrooms, a good rule of thumb is to let them alone in the frying pan. Bumping them around too much will cause them to release too much moisture, and they will end up stewing, not browning.

1. Place the quinoa in a small saucepan, add the water and bring to a boil. Reduce heat to medium-low and cook covered for 15 to 18 minutes. The quinoa is done when the grains are translucent and all the water has been absorbed. Fluff with a fork, remove from heat and let stand covered for 5 to 10 minutes.

2. Meanwhile, heat a large frying pan over medium heat. Add the oil and mushrooms. Let the mushrooms sit and brown for about 3 to 5 minutes before stirring. Let brown for another 3 to 5 minutes (see sidebar).

3. Add the onions and garlic and sauté about 3 to 5 minutes, until lightly browned.

4. Add the carrots, thyme, rosemary and pepper. Stir well. Add ¼ cup (60 mL) broth, cover and cook for 3 to 5 minutes, stirring occasionally.

5. Add the frozen edamame and stir until they turn bright green.

6. Stir in cooked quinoa. Crumble the goat feta in and gently mix. Add the rest of the broth (¼ cup/60 mL). Stir in, cover and reduce heat to low. Cook for 3 to 5 minutes, or until the cheese has melted and the edamame are cooked through.

Makes 5 cups (1.25 L) • One serving = 1¼ cups (310 mL)

Nutrition per serving

243 calories	11 g total fat	4 g saturated fat
9 mg cholesterol	162 mg sodium	23 g carbohydrates
5 g fibre	7 g sugars	12 g protein

Excellent source of vitamin A.

This delicious all-in-one main course is a treasure chest of nutrients. One serving provides an excellent source of vitamin A, folate, vitamin C, magnesium, iron and zinc. So get out your frying pan or wok and start making dinner.

YEAR ROUND

Diana Rodel, PHEc

Cashew Vegetable Stir-Fry

1. **QUINOA:** Place the quinoa in a medium saucepan, add the water and bring to a boil. Reduce heat to medium-low and cook covered for 15 to 20 minutes. The quinoa is done when the grains are translucent and all the water has been absorbed. Fluff with a fork, remove from heat and add 1 tsp (5 mL) of the garlic and herb salt-free seasoning. Fluff with a fork again. Let stand covered.

2. **STIR-FRY SAUCE:** Meanwhile, in a small bowl, whisk together the stir-fry sauce ingredients, including the remaining garlic and herb salt-free seasoning. Set aside.

3. **STIR-FRY:** To a large wok or frying pan over medium heat, add 1 Tbsp (15 mL) of the oil. Sauté the onion, garlic and ginger for 5 minutes. Remove half and gently fold into the cooked quinoa. Replace lid on saucepan.

4. Add the remaining 1 Tbsp (15 mL) of oil to the wok. Add the broccoli, pepper, carrot, corn and water chestnuts. Continue to stir-fry for 5 to 7 minutes, or until the broccoli is tender crisp.

5. Whisk the stir-fry sauce again and then add it to the vegetables. Cook until the sauce bubbles and is clear, then add the cashews. Stir in well.

6. Fold 2 Tbsp (30 mL) of the chopped cilantro into the cooked quinoa.

7. **TO SERVE:** Spoon a heaping ½ cup (125 mL) of the cooked quinoa onto each plate. Top with 1¾ cups of the cooked vegetables and nuts (about a quarter of the mixture), and sprinkle with chopped cilantro.

Makes 4 servings • One serving = a heaping ½ cup (125 mL) quinoa with 1¾ cups (435 mL) stir-fry

Nutrition per serving

489 calories	22 g total fat	3 g saturated fat
0 mg cholesterol	511 mg sodium	68 g carbohydrates
8 g fibre	20 g sugars	13 g protein

Excellent source of vitamin A, folate, vitamin C, magnesium, iron and zinc.

QUINOA

¾ cup (185 mL)	quinoa, rinsed and drained
1¼ cups (310 mL)	water
2 tsp (10 mL)	garlic and herb salt-free seasoning blend, divided

STIR-FRY SAUCE

1 Tbsp (15 mL)	cornstarch
2 Tbsp (30 mL)	liquid honey
3 Tbsp (45 mL)	sodium-reduced soy sauce
¾ cup (185 mL)	vegetable broth
2 Tbsp (30 mL)	orange juice
1 Tbsp (15 mL)	apple cider vinegar
½ tsp (2 mL)	extra spicy salt-free seasoning blend

STIR-FRY

2 Tbsp (30 mL)	canola oil, divided
1	medium onion, cut in half and thinly sliced into half-moon slices
4	cloves garlic, minced
2 Tbsp (30 mL)	finely chopped fresh ginger
4 cups (1 L)	broccoli florets (about 1 small bunch)
1	medium red pepper, cut into thin strips
1	large carrot, scrubbed well and thinly sliced into coin-sized pieces
½ cup (125 mL)	frozen corn, no need to thaw
1 can (8 oz/227 g)	water chestnuts, drained, rinsed and thinly sliced
¾ cup (185 mL)	whole unsalted roasted cashews
¼ cup (60 mL)	chopped fresh cilantro, divided

Tofu Dinner with
Asian Flavours

If you love Chinese takeout, here's a much healthier version that's a real winner in the flavour department. NOTE: Sriracha hot chili sauce, hoisin and dark sesame oil can be found in the Asian foods section of larger grocery stores. If you don't have any luck finding Sriracha, you may substitute Kikkoman Thai-style chili sauce.

FALL, WINTER and SPRING

Bridget Wilson, PHEc

Tofu Dinner with Asian Flavours

1. Heat a large non-stick frying pan over medium heat. Add the oil and onions and sauté for 4 minutes, until the onion has softened.

2. Add the ginger and garlic and sauté for another minute.

3. Stir in the broth, quinoa, tofu, soy sauce, hoisin sauce, sesame oil and hot chilli sauce. Bring to a boil, then reduce heat to low and simmer covered for 18 to 20 minutes.

4. Stir in the carrots and peppers. Return to a simmer and cook covered for another 5 to 10 minutes, until the vegetables have softened.

5. **TO SERVE:** Toss in the green onions, remove from heat and let stand covered for 5 minutes before serving.

Makes 6 cups (1.5 L) • **One serving = 1½ cups (375 mL)**

2 tsp (10 mL)	canola oil
1	large onion, chopped
3 Tbsp (45 mL)	minced fresh ginger
3	cloves garlic, minced
2 cups (500 mL)	vegetable broth
1 cup (250 mL)	quinoa, rinsed and drained
12 oz (360 g)	extra-firm tofu, cut into ½-inch (1 cm) cubes
2 Tbsp (30 mL)	sodium-reduced soy sauce
1 Tbsp (15 mL)	hoisin sauce
1 Tbsp (15 mL)	dark sesame oil
1 Tbsp (15 mL)	Sriracha hot chili sauce
1	medium carrot, scrubbed well and julienned (see page 8)
1	red pepper, cut in thin strips
4	green onions, thinly sliced

Nutrition per serving

365 calories	12 g total fat	1 g saturated fat
0 mg cholesterol	639 mg sodium	48 g carbohydrates
6 g fibre	8 g sugars	16 g protein

Excellent source of vitamin A, vitamin C, magnesium and iron.

This hearty, family-friendly recipe —*is it a soup or a stew?*—will tickle your taste buds. The sweetness from the dried apricots adds that Moroccan flavour, plus a hit of disease-lowering beta carotene. Factor in the amount of vegetables in every bite and this is a veggie winner.

Moroccan Vegetable Stew

2 tsp (10 mL)	extra virgin olive oil
1	onion, chopped
1½-inch (4 cm) piece	peeled fresh ginger, grated
3	cloves garlic, minced
1½ tsp (7 mL)	curry powder
1 tsp (5 mL)	ground cinnamon
6 cups (1.5 L)	vegetable broth
1 can (19 oz/540 mL)	low-sodium chickpeas, well rinsed and drained
1 can (14 oz/398 mL)	diced tomatoes, no salt added
½ cup (125 mL)	red quinoa, rinsed and drained
2	medium carrots, scrubbed well and cut into ¼-inch (6 mm) slices
¼ cup (60 mL)	sliced dried apricots
2	medium zucchini, quartered lengthwise and then cut into ½-inch (1 cm) slices
1 cup (250 mL)	kale, stems removed, leaves only, chopped into bite-sized pieces
1 cup (250 mL)	frozen peas, no need to thaw
½ cup (125 mL)	whole almonds, coarsely chopped

1. Heat a large stock pot over medium heat. Add the oil, onion, ginger, garlic, curry powder and cinnamon. Sauté for 3 to 5 minutes, or until the onion has softened.

2. Add the broth, chickpeas, tomatoes, quinoa, carrots and apricots. Bring to a boil, then reduce heat to low and simmer, covered, for 15 minutes.

3. Add the zucchini and continue simmering covered for another 5 to 10 minutes, or until the zucchini is soft but not mushy.

4. Add the kale and peas. Heat until the kale has wilted and the peas are hot. Add the almonds and stir well.

5. **TO SERVE:** Ladle the stew into soup bowls. Serve with a glass of milk or organic soy beverage to up the protein count.

Makes 10 to 12 cups (2.5 to 3 L) • One serving = 1½ cups (375 mL)

Nutrition per serving

237 calories	7 g total fat	1 g saturated fat
0 mg cholesterol	584 mg sodium	36 g carbohydrates
8 g fibre	11 g sugars	10 g protein

Excellent source of vitamin A.

Moroccan Vegetable Stew

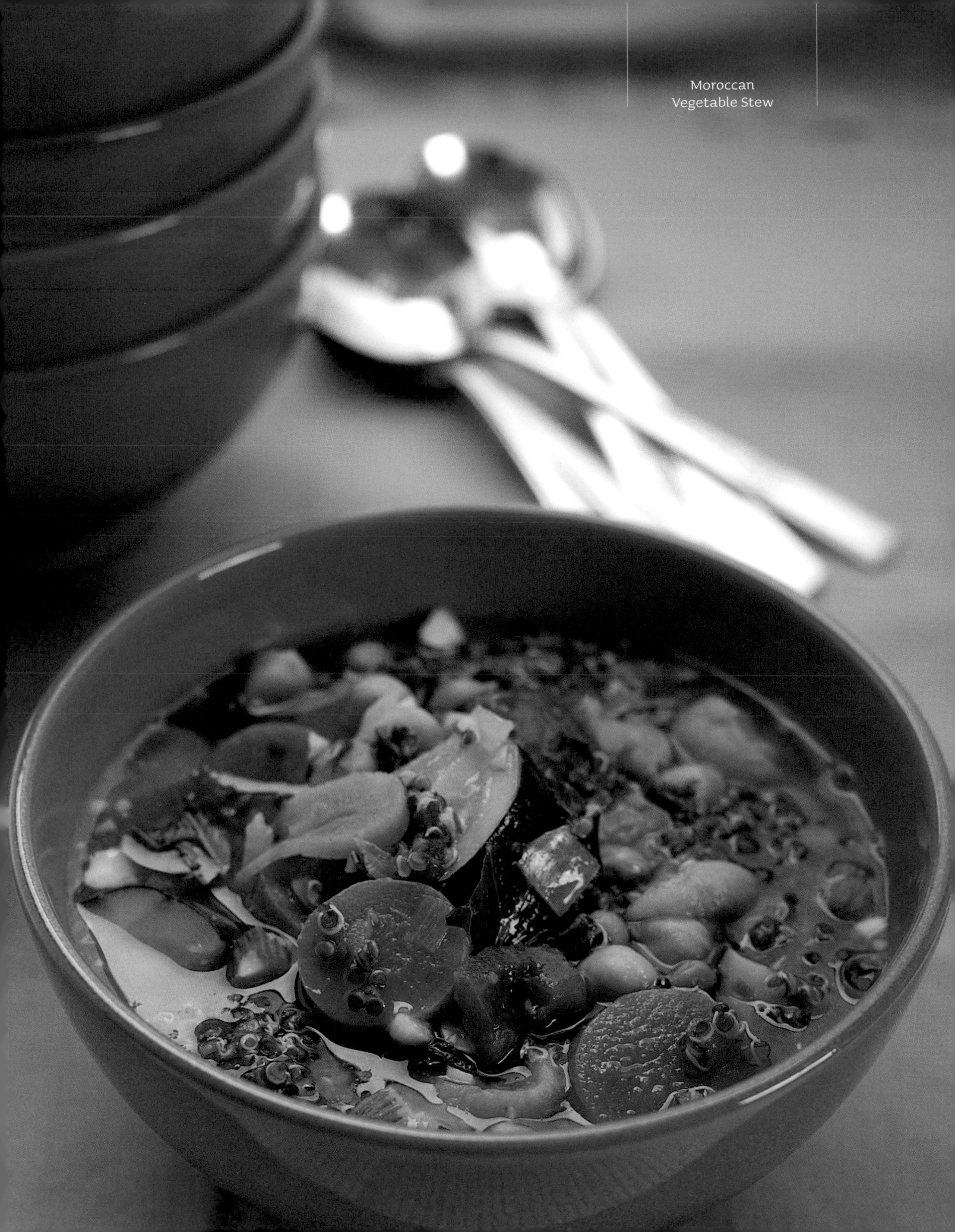

YEAR ROUND

Teresa Makarewicz,
PHEc

In a hurry, and who isn't these days? Have some cooked quinoa in the fridge? What about a bag of frozen veggies? If you answered yes to any of these questions—this is the recipe for you. NOTE: To kick this recipe up a notch, use exotic mixed frozen vegetables—California or Asian style.

In-a-Hurry Stir-Fry with Cooked Quinoa

1 Tbsp (15 mL)	canola oil
3	cloves garlic, minced
1	onion, diced
1 tsp (5 mL)	ground cumin
Pinch	cayenne pepper (optional)
2½ cups (625 mL)	cooked quinoa (see pages 5–6)
2 cups (500 mL)	frozen mixed vegetables, thawed (see sidebar)
1 Tbsp (15 mL)	sodium-reduced soy sauce
½ cup + 2 Tbsp (155 mL)	roasted unsalted cashews, chopped

To thaw frozen veggies, place them in a strainer and rinse *briefly* under hot water. Drain and then use in the recipe.

1. Set your timer to 15 minutes. Three, two, one . . . *go!*

2. In a large non-stick frying pan over medium heat, heat the oil. Add the garlic, onion, cumin and cayenne pepper (if using). Sauté for 5 minutes, or until the onion has softened.

3. Stir in the cooked quinoa and thawed vegetables. Sauté for 4 minutes, or until heated through.

4. **TO SERVE:** Sprinkle with soy sauce in the pan. Stir quickly and serve sprinkled with cashews. *Stop!* From start to finish, the time should be about 15 minutes.

Makes about 5 cups (1.25 L) • One serving = 1 cup (250 mL)

Nutrition per serving

492 calories	15 g total fat	2 g saturated fat
0 mg cholesterol	135 mg sodium	76 g carbohydrates
12 g fibre	7 g sugars	16 g protein

Excellent source of riboflavin, folate, magnesium and iron.

124   THE VEGETARIAN'S COMPLETE QUINOA COOKBOOK

Another quick dinner idea? Got 30 minutes? This flavourful, nutrient-dense and economical dish is the answer. It uses only a few simple ingredients that you are likely to have on hand. NOTE: Try using seasoned canned tomatoes for a more robust flavour.

YEAR ROUND

Diane O'Shea, PHEc

Quinoa with Tomatoes and Fresh Herbs

1. Heat a large saucepan over medium heat. Add the oil and onion and sauté for about 3 minutes, or until the onion is starting to soften.

2. Add the garlic and pepper and sauté for about another minute.

3. Add the canned tomatoes and bring to a boil, scraping any bits that stick to the bottom of the pan.

4. Stir in the quinoa and return to a boil, stirring occasionally. Reduce heat to low. Cover and simmer for 20 to 25 minutes, or until the quinoa is tender and the liquid is almost absorbed.

5. Remove from heat and stir in the parsley and basil. Cover and let stand for 5 minutes.

6. **TO SERVE:** Fluff with a fork. Season with more pepper, if desired. Sprinkle with the Parmesan cheese.

Makes 4 cups (1 L) • One serving = 1 cup (250 mL)

1 Tbsp (15 mL)	extra virgin olive oil
1	onion, diced
3	cloves garlic, minced
¼ tsp (1 mL)	freshly ground black pepper
1 can (28 oz/796 mL)	diced tomatoes
1 cup (250 mL)	quinoa, rinsed and drained
¼ cup (60 mL)	finely chopped fresh parsley
¼ cup (60 mL)	fresh basil, chiffonade (see page 8)
½ cup (125 mL)	freshly grated Parmesan cheese

Nutrition per serving

301 calories	10 g total fat	3 g saturated fat
11 mg cholesterol	603 mg sodium	42 g carbohydrates
5 g fibre	7 g sugars	13 g protein

Excellent source of vitamin C and iron.

When it comes to cheese-stuffed pasta shells that your kids will love, do we have a recipe for you. This comfort dish has all the elements for a cozy supper, so dig in. Leftovers are even better the next day. NOTE: You can find shells made with brown rice and quinoa in larger health food stores.

Cheese Jumbo "Pasta" Shells

1 Tbsp (15 mL)	canola oil
1	onion, finely chopped
1	red pepper, finely chopped
2	small, zucchini, coarsely grated
½ tsp (2 mL)	balsamic vinegar
½ tsp (2 mL)	dried rosemary, crushed
¼ tsp (1 mL)	freshly ground black pepper
24	jumbo brown rice shells
1½ cups (375 mL)	cooked quinoa made with vegetable broth (see pages 5–6)
1	omega-3 egg
1½ cups (375 mL)	low-fat ricotta
½ cup (125 mL)	grated Parmesan cheese
2½ cups (625 mL)	low-sodium tomato pasta sauce, divided
½ cup (125 mL)	part-skim mozzarella

1. Preheat the oven to 375°F (190°C). Lightly grease a 9- × 13-inch (3.5 L) shallow casserole dish with canola oil or use wet parchment paper (see page 10).

2. In a large frying pan, heat the oil over medium heat. Add the onion, red pepper, zucchini, vinegar, rosemary and pepper. Cook for about 10 minutes, stirring often, until the onion has softened and the liquid has evaporated. Transfer to a large bowl. Let stand until cool.

3. Meanwhile, in a large saucepan, bring 16 cups (4 L) water and ½ tsp (2 mL) salt to a boil. Add the shells and stir. Return to a boil and boil uncovered for 10 to 12 minutes, stirring occasionally, until the shells are tender but firm (al dente). Drain. Rinse with cold water. Drain well.

4. Add the cooked quinoa to the onion mixture and stir in until well incorporated.

5. In a small bowl, beat together the egg, ricotta and Parmesan cheese. Stir into the quinoa mixture.

6. Spread ½ cup (125 mL) of the pasta sauce on the bottom of the prepared baking dish. Fill each pasta shell with a heaping 1 Tbsp (15 mL) of the quinoa mixture. (For easy stuffing, use a teaspoon to load up the shell.) Arrange the pasta shells in a single layer over the sauce.

7. Spoon the remaining pasta sauce over top of the filled pasta shells.

8. Sprinkle the mozzarella cheese over top. Tear off a piece of foil a little bit bigger than the pan. Lightly spray the inside of the foil with canola oil spray and cover the pan loosely. Bake for 40 minutes. Remove and discard the foil. Bake for an additional 15 minutes, or until the cheese starts to turn golden brown. Let stand for 5 minutes before serving.

Makes 8 servings • One serving = 3 jumbo shells with ⅛ of the sauce

Nutrition per serving

395 calories	10 g total fat	3 g saturated fat
44 mg cholesterol	455 mg sodium	61 g carbohydrates
6 g fibre	11 g sugars	16 g protein

Comfort foods are always crowd-pleasers, so don't plan on any leftovers when you serve this dish. BONUS: The soluble fibre from the beans and the eggplant can help lower your cholesterol.

FALL and WINTER

Emily Campbell, SHEA
student member

Sweet Potato, Eggplant and Feta Quinoa

1. Heat a large non-stick frying pan over medium heat. Add the oil and onion and sauté 3 to 5 minutes, until the onion has softened.

2. Add the garlic, cinnamon and cumin. Sauté for another minute.

3. Add the sweet potato, eggplant, beans and 1 cup (250 mL) of the broth. Gently stir together. Bring to a boil, then reduce heat to medium-low and simmer covered, stirring occasionally, 20 to 25 minutes, until the sweet potato is tender.

4. Meanwhile, cook the quinoa. Place the quinoa in a large saucepan, add the remaining 2 cups (500 mL) of broth and bring to a boil. Reduce heat to medium-low and cook covered for 15 to 20 minutes. The quinoa is done when the grains are translucent and all the liquid has been absorbed. Fluff with a fork, remove from heat and let stand covered for 5 to 10 minutes.

5. Gently fold the quinoa into the vegetable/bean mixture.

6. **TO SERVE:** Sprinkle each serving with 1 Tbsp (15 mL) of the crumbled feta.

Makes 9 cups (2.25 L) • One serving = 1½ cups (375 mL)

1 Tbsp (15 mL)	extra virgin olive oil
1	medium onion, diced
1	large clove garlic, minced
1 tsp (5 mL)	cinnamon
½ tsp (2 mL)	ground cumin
1	large sweet potato (1 lb/500 g) scrubbed well and chopped into ½-inch (1 cm) pieces
1	small eggplant (½ lb/250 g) scrubbed well and chopped into ½-inch (1 cm) pieces
1 can (19 oz/540 mL)	black beans, well rinsed and drained
3 cups (750 mL)	vegetable broth, divided
1 cup (250 mL)	quinoa, rinsed and drained
6 Tbsp (90 mL)	crumbled goat feta

Nutrition per serving

318 calories	7 g total fat	2 g saturated fat
9 mg cholesterol	389 mg sodium	54 g carbohydrates
10 g fibre	8 g sugars	11 g protein

Excellent source of vitamin A, magnesium and iron.

Give a cheer for the slow cooker! This recipe is great for those hectic days when you are driving one child to hockey practice and the other to a music lesson. Leftovers are fabulous the next day; it's a great big pot of love. NOTE: Catelli's Healthy Harvest line features whole-grain lasagna noodles. Be sure to choose a pasta sauce that lists tomatoes as the first ingredient.

Slow Cooker Vegetarian Lasagna

1 can (19 oz/540 mL)	mixed beans, well rinsed and drained
2⅔ cups (650 mL)	pasta sauce
⅔ cup (160 mL)	canned diced tomatoes
¾ cup (185 mL)	quinoa, rinsed and drained
2 tsp (10 mL)	Italian seasoning
1 tsp (5 mL)	dried oregano leaves
8	uncooked lasagna noodles, preferably 100% whole grain
1 cup (250 mL)	sliced white or cremini mushrooms
2 cups (500 mL)	cooked chopped spinach leaves, well drained (or 10 oz/300 g frozen chopped spinach, thawed and well drained)
2 cups (500 mL)	fat-free cottage cheese
2 cups (500 mL)	grated mozzarella cheese

1. Grease a 6-quart (6 L) slow cooker with canola oil.

2. In a medium bowl, combine the mixed beans, pasta sauce, diced tomatoes, quinoa (yes, it's uncooked!), Italian seasoning and oregano. Mix well and set aside.

3. Place one layer of noodles on the bottom of the slow cooker, breaking to fit. (See Photo 1.)

4. Top with half of the bean–pasta sauce–quinoa mixture. (See Photo 2.)

5. Top with half of the mushrooms, and half of the spinach. (See Photo 3.)

6. Top with half of the cottage cheese. (See Photo 4.)

7. Repeat the layers: noodles, bean–pasta sauce–quinoa mixture, mushrooms and spinach, cottage cheese.

8. Top with all of the mozzarella cheese. (See Photo 5.)

9. Cover and cook on Low for 5 hours. (See Photo 6.)

10. **TO SERVE:** Let sit for 5 minutes, then scoop out servings. Serve with a mixed green salad.

Makes 10 servings • One serving = ¹⁄₁₀ of the lasagna

Nutrition per serving

322 calories	6 g total fat	3 g saturated fat
17 mg cholesterol	579 mg sodium	47 g carbohydrates
7 g fibre	7 g sugars	22 g protein

Excellent source of folate, vitamin D and iron.

Slow Cooker
Vegetarian Lasagna

Risotto is all about creaminess and cheese. Make sure you're using the real thing when it comes to Parmesan. Parmesan Reggiano has a strong flavour and is the perfect choice for this dish. NOTE: To wash asparagus, snap or cut off the woody bottom of each stalk and discard. Chop remaining part into 1-inch (2.5 cm) pieces for this recipe.

Asparagus and Parmesan "Risotto"

1 Tbsp (15 mL)	extra virgin olive oil
4	large shallots, diced
3	cloves garlic, minced
1 cup (250 mL)	red quinoa, rinsed and drained
2¼ cups (560 mL)	vegetable broth
2 cups (500 mL)	chopped asparagus
2 Tbsp (30 mL)	quinoa flour (see page 7)
½ cup (125 mL)	freshly grated Parmesan Reggiano

1. Heat a large saucepan over medium heat. Add the oil and shallots. Sauté for 5 minutes, until the shallots are soft and golden brown.

2. Add the garlic and sauté for another minute.

3. Add the quinoa and broth. Bring to a boil, then reduce heat to medium-low and cook covered for 15 to 18 minutes. Stir and add the asparagus.

4. Return to a boil and cook covered for 5 to 10 minutes, or until the asparagus is cooked to your liking.

5. Stir in the quinoa flour, return to a boil and cook uncovered for another minute.

6. **TO SERVE:** Add the cheese, stir well and serve immediately. Goes well with a mixed green salad.

Makes 4 cups (1 L) • One serving = 1 cup (250 mL)

Nutrition per serving

309 calories	10 g total fat	3 g saturated fat
11 mg cholesterol	465 mg sodium	43 g carbohydrates
6 g fibre	4 g sugars	14 g protein

Excellent source of folate, iron and zinc.

This low-calorie, family-friendly main course is great for vegetarians as well as their friends who aren't. It might even sway the latter to start eating meatless more often. Here's hoping.

YEAR ROUND

Laura Katz, SHEA
student member

Pesto Primavera Supper

1. Heat a large saucepan over medium heat. Add the oil and shallots and sauté for 5 to 7 minutes, or until the shallots are translucent.

2. Add the carrots, yellow pepper, Italian seasoning and pepper. Continue sautéing for 5 minutes, or until the yellow pepper is soft.

3. Add the quinoa, broth, tomato sauce and pesto. Bring to a boil and stir. Reduce heat to low and simmer covered for 10 to 15 minutes, or until the quinoa is almost cooked.

4. Add the broccoli and kidney beans. Return to a boil, then reduce heat to low and simmer covered for another 5 minutes.

5. **TO SERVE:** Add the spinach and stir until wilted. Stir in the cheese and serve immediately.

Makes 7 cups (1.75 L) • **One serving = 1 cup (250 mL)**

1 Tbsp (15 mL)	extra virgin olive oil
3	shallots, diced
2	medium carrots, scrubbed well and sliced into thin coins
1	yellow pepper, diced
2 tsp (10 mL)	Italian seasoning
¼ tsp (1 mL)	freshly ground black pepper
½ cup (125 mL)	quinoa, rinsed and drained
1 cup (250 mL)	vegetable broth
1 cup (250 mL)	flavoured tomato sauce (your choice)
2 Tbsp (30 mL)	homemade or commercial pesto
2 cups (500 mL)	broccoli, chopped into bite-sized pieces
1 can (19 oz/540 mL)	red kidney beans, well rinsed and drained
2½ cups (625 mL)	packed baby spinach
¾ cup (185 mL)	grated Parmesan cheese

Nutrition per serving

245 calories	8 g total fat	2 g saturated fat
7 mg cholesterol	579 mg sodium	32 g carbohydrates
7 g fibre	7 g sugars	12 g protein

Excellent source of vitamin C and iron.

Black Bean Bake with
Feta Crumb Topping

This easy-to-make casserole is a great make-ahead recipe that scores big with kids, young and old. NOTE: No food processor? Use frozen whole wheat bread and grate on the coarse side of a box cheese grater. To lower the sodium, use canned unsalted black beans.

YEAR ROUND

Teresa Makarewicz, PHEc

Black Bean Bake with Feta Crumb Topping

1. Preheat the oven to 375°F (190°C). Lightly grease an 8-cup (2 L) shallow baking dish with canola oil.

2. Place the quinoa in a medium saucepan, add the broth and bay leaf and bring to a boil. Reduce heat to medium-low and cook covered for 15 to 20 minutes. The quinoa is done when the grains are translucent and all the liquid has been absorbed. Fluff with a fork, remove from heat and let stand covered for 5 to 10 minutes. Discard bay leaf.

3. Meanwhile, in a large non-stick frying pan, heat the oil over medium heat. Add the garlic, onion, oregano and red pepper flakes. Cook, stirring occasionally, about 5 minutes, until the onion has softened.

4. Add the red peppers and cook for about 3 minutes, or until the peppers are just softened.

5. Add the canned tomatoes and beans. Stir in well and bring to a boil. Reduce heat to low and simmer uncovered for 5 minutes, or until most of the liquid has evaporated.

6. Remove from heat and add the cooked quinoa and ¼ cup (60 mL) of the parsley. Transfer to the prepared baking dish.

7. Pulse bread in a food processor until it looks like soft crumbs. In a small bowl, combine the breadcrumbs, crumbled feta and remaining parsley. Sprinkle over the quinoa mixture.

8. Bake in the centre of the oven for 20 to 25 minutes, or until topping is golden brown.

Makes 8 cups (2 L) • **One serving = 1½ cups (375 mL)**

¾ cup (185 mL)	quinoa, rinsed and drained
1¼ cups (310 mL)	vegetable broth
1	bay leaf
1 Tbsp (15 mL)	canola oil
4	cloves garlic, minced
1	onion, diced
1 Tbsp (15 mL)	dried oregano leaves
½ tsp (2 mL)	red pepper flakes, or to taste
1	sweet red pepper, coarsely chopped
1 can (28 oz/796 mL)	diced tomatoes, no salt added
1 can (19 oz/540 mL)	black beans, well rinsed and drained
½ cup (125 mL)	chopped flat-leaf parsley, divided
2 slices	100% whole-grain whole wheat bread
1 cup (250 mL)	finely crumbled goat feta

Nutrition per serving

309 calories	10 g total fat	4 g saturated fat
23 mg cholesterol	606 mg sodium	43 g carbohydrates
8 g fibre	7 g sugars	13 g protein

Excellent source of vitamin C and iron.

YEAR ROUND

Andrea Villneff, OHEA
provisional member

Fire up your oven and heat up your pizza stone: here's a pizza that's made with quinoa flour. Serve this with a glass of milk or organic soy beverage to bump up the protein. NOTE: You can find psyllium husks at most larger grocery stores that have a health food section.

Pesto Pizza

1 cup (250 mL)	quinoa flour (see page 7)
1 tsp (5 mL)	psyllium husk
¾ cup (185 mL)	water
2 Tbsp (30 mL)	homemade or commercial pesto
½ cup (125 mL)	grated part-skim mozzarella
½	shallot, thinly sliced,
1	large tomato, thinly sliced
½ tsp (2 mL)	dried oregano leaves, or to taste

1. Preheat the oven to 400°F (200°C). Line a large baking sheet, a pizza pan or a pizza stone with parchment paper.

2. Whisk together the quinoa flour and psyllium husks in a large bowl. Slowly whisk in the water until the mixture looks like a thick batter.

3. Spread the batter onto the prepared pan into an 8-inch (20 cm) circle.

4. Bake in the centre of the oven for 20 minutes.

5. Remove from the oven and gently flip the crust over so the browned side is on the top.

6. Bake for another 5 minutes. Remove from the oven and spread the pesto over the thin crust. Sprinkle evenly with the cheese. Distribute the shallot evenly on the crust, cover with tomato slices, and sprinkle with oregano.

7. Bake in the centre of the oven for 5 to 10 minutes, or until the toppings are warm and the cheese has melted.

Makes 4 servings • One serving = ¼ of the pizza

Nutrition per serving

208 calories	7 g total fat	2 g saturated fat
10 mg cholesterol	176 mg sodium	25 g carbohydrates
5 g fibre	2 g sugars	9 g protein

Excellent source of vitamin A.

This crêpe recipe can be used for the Spinach Lasagna Crêpes (page 136) or filled with your favourite savoury filling. See page 171 for "Tips for making perfect crêpes." NOTE: 2 cups (500 mL) of fresh baby spinach will yield about ½ cup (125 mL) of cooked drained spinach.

YEAR ROUND

Deb Campbell, PHEc

Spinach Crêpes

1. In a food processor fitted with a metal blade, process the flour, egg, oil and soy beverage for 10 to 15 seconds, until smooth (batter must be lump free). Add the cooked, drained spinach and process for another 10 seconds. Refrigerate batter for at least 30 minutes before cooking. This allows bubbles to dissipate and gives a nicer finished product.

2. Very lightly grease a small (7-inch/18 cm) frying pan with canola oil. NOTE: A lightly seasoned pan will give you a more uniform crêpe pancake.

3. Spoon a scant 3 Tbsp (45 mL) of batter into the pan and rotate the pan around to evenly coat the bottom. Try not to run the batter up the sides of the pan, as this will make the edges overcrisp. After 30 seconds, turn over the crêpe. It will be lightly browned on both sides and will be flexible (for folding or rolling).

4. Place the cooked crêpes on parchment paper to cool. They can be frozen at this point for later use (see sidebar). Or use for Spinach Lasagna Crêpes (page 136).

Makes 12 crêpes • One serving = 1 crêpe

¾ cup (185 mL)	quinoa flour (see page 7)
1	omega-3 egg
¼ cup (60 mL)	canola oil
1 cup (250 mL)	organic unsweetened soy beverage
½ cup (125 mL)	cooked and well-drained spinach

Freeze crêpes in small amounts for easy use. Place a small piece of parchment between the layers, wrap in clear plastic wrap, and freeze for up to 1 month.

Nutrition per serving

83 calories	6 g total fat	0 g saturated fat
16 mg cholesterol	15 mg sodium	6 g carbohydrates
1 g fibre	0 g sugars	2 g protein

This entrée has all the traditional flavours of lasagna. The dish can be frozen after the rolls are made. Then, on serving day, simply add the sauce and grated mozzarella cheese and bake in the oven until golden brown and bubbly. NOTE: Although optional, Italian seasoning adds a big hit of flavour.

Spinach Lasagna Crêpes

1 recipe	Spinach Crêpes (page 135)
2 cups (500 mL)	1% cottage cheese
1	omega-3 egg
¼ cup (60 mL)	grated Parmesan cheese
1 can (14 oz/398 mL)	tomato sauce, no salt added
1 Tbsp (15 mL)	Italian seasoning (optional)
1 cup (250 mL)	grated part-skim mozzarella

1. Prepare a recipe of Spinach Crêpes. Once cooked, set aside.

2. Preheat the oven to 350°F (175°C). Lightly grease a 9- × 13-inch (3.5 L) casserole dish with canola oil or line with wet parchment paper (see page 10).

3. In a medium bowl, combine the cottage cheese, egg and Parmesan cheese with a spoon.

4. Place a crêpe on a clean cutting board or a large plate. Place a heaping 2 Tbsp (30 mL) of the cheese mixture one-third in from edge. Spread out the mixture in a log formation and tightly roll up the crêpe. Place it seam side down in the prepared dish. Continue to fill the crêpes and place them in the dish. You may have to stack them. No worries—they'll all taste great.

5. In a medium bowl, mix together the tomato sauce and Italian seasoning (if using). Pour the sauce over the crêpes and sprinkle the grated mozzarella cheese overtop.

6. Bake for 35 to 40 minutes, until golden and bubbly.

7. **TO SERVE:** Let stand for 5 minutes to set before serving. Serve with sliced cucumbers or a Greek salad.

Makes 12 crêpes • One serving = 2 crêpes

Nutrition per serving

340 calories	18 g total fat	5 g saturated fat
85 mg cholesterol	389 mg sodium	22 g carbohydrates
3 g fibre	7 g sugars	22 g protein

Excellent source of vitamin D and calcium.

This versatile, quiche-like dish makes a delicious brunch or a simple supper any time. The choice of vegetables and cheese can be varied according to what you have on hand. Try making the dish with spinach, cooked broccoli, onions or sweet peppers. Vary the cheese to suit your taste.

YEAR ROUND

Wendi Hiebert, PHEc

Kale and Feta Bake

1. Preheat the oven to 350°F (175°C). Lightly spray a 9-inch (23 cm) square baking pan with canola oil spray or, for an easier cleanup, line the pan with wet parchment paper (see page 10).

2. Spread the kale over the bottom of the dish. Sprinkle the crumbled feta and sun-dried tomatoes over top.

3. In a large bowl, whisk the eggs lightly. Add the milk and quinoa; whisk to combine. Carefully pour the quinoa mixture over the kale, feta and sun-dried tomatoes. With a fork, poke the kale so it is submerged under the egg mixture, and make sure most of the quinoa is submerged as well. Just do your best!

4. Bake in the centre of the oven just until set, about 35 to 40 minutes.

5. **TO SERVE:** Remove from the oven and let stand for 5 minutes before serving. Any leftovers can be reheated in the microwave the next day.

Makes 6 servings • One serving = ⅙ of the cooked recipe

3 cups (750 mL)	well-packed, finely chopped kale leaves, stems removed
1 cup (250 mL)	crumbled goat feta
¼ cup (60 mL)	chopped sun-dried tomatoes, oil-packed, well-drained
8	omega-3 eggs
1¼ cups (310 mL)	skim milk
½ cup (125 mL)	quinoa, rinsed and drained

Vegetarians have a hard time getting omega-3 fatty acids into their diets. Omega-3 is an essential fatty acid that the body cannot produce on its own and that contributes to heart and brain health. Vegetarian sources of omega-3 fatty acids are canola oil, walnuts, flaxseed, chia seeds and omega-3 eggs. We recommend using omega-3 eggs in all the recipes that call for eggs.

Nutrition per serving

256 calories	14 g total fat	5 g saturated fat
277 mg cholesterol	403 mg sodium	18 g carbohydrates
2 g fibre	4 g sugars	17 g protein

Are your vegetarian kids fans of Dr. Seuss? Need to make green eggs minus the ham? Purée the eggs and spinach before adding the other ingredients. Your kids will love the result, and you can rest assured that they got a great boost of B vitamins.

Energy Omelette

3	omega-3 eggs
¼ cup (60 mL)	coarsely chopped and tightly packed baby spinach
¼ cup (60 mL)	cooked quinoa (see pages 5–6)
1 tsp (5 mL)	chopped red pepper
1 tsp (5 mL)	diced onion
1 tsp (5 mL)	ground flaxseed
2 tsp (10 mL)	canola oil
2 Tbsp (30 mL)	extra-old grated cheddar cheese

1. In a medium bowl, lightly beat the eggs. Stir in the spinach, cooked quinoa, red pepper, onion and flaxseed.

2. Heat a large non-stick frying pan over medium heat. Add the oil and pour in the egg mixture, slowly swirling the pan to cook evenly.

3. Cover with a lid and cook until the omelette is firm, about 1½ to 2 minutes. Sprinkle the cheese on the top and let melt. Fold over in the pan, using a flipper, and cut the omelette in half.

4. **TO SERVE:** Transfer to a plate and serve immediately.

Makes 1 omelette • One serving = ½ of the omelette

Nutrition per serving

266 calories	16 g total fat	3 g saturated fat
294 mg cholesterol	149 mg sodium	17 g carbohydrates
3 g fibre	1 g sugars	14 g protein

Excellent source of riboflavin, vitamin B12 and folate.

It's always handy to have some cooked quinoa in the fridge ready to go for quick and easy dinner ideas. Serve this omelette with a leafy green salad, a slice of 100% whole-grain bread and a glass of milk or organic soy beverage. Dinner can be on the table in about 15 minutes.

SPRING

Anna Shier,
OHEA student
member

Asparagus Rosemary Omelette

1. In a large bowl, using a whisk, beat the eggs until slightly fluffy. Add the cooked quinoa, asparagus, rosemary and pepper and mix well.

2. Heat a large non-stick frying pan over medium heat. Add the oil and pour in the egg mixture, slowly swirling the pan and lifting the edges of the omelette to allow the uncooked portions to go to the edges and cook.

3. When there is only a small amount of liquid egg remaining in the middle, about 3 to 5 minutes depending on your stove, add the cheese, cover and cook until the omelette is cooked through and the cheese is soft and slightly melted.

4. **TO SERVE:** Gently fold the omelette in half in the pan and flip onto a clean cutting board. Cut into quarters and serve immediately. Goes well with a mixed green salad.

Makes 4 servings • One serving = ¼ of the omelette

4	omega-3 eggs
½ cup (125 mL)	cooked quinoa made with water (see pages 5–6)
4	medium asparagus stalks, woody end removed, chopped into ¼-inch (6 mm) pieces
1½ tsp (7 mL)	dried rosemary leaves or 1 Tbsp (15 mL) fresh rosemary leaves, chopped
	Freshly ground pepper to taste
1½ tsp (7 mL)	canola oil
½ cup (125 mL)	crumbled goat feta

Nutrition per serving

167 calories	11 g total fat	5 g saturated fat
207 mg cholesterol	266 mg sodium	7 g carbohydrates
1 g fibre	1 g sugars	10 g protein

Excellent source of riboflavin, folate and vitamin B12.

Frittatas are baked omelettes that tend to have many more
additions than a regular omelette and are totally worth the extra
chopping. NOTE: For a sweeter flavour, roast the garlic in the oven
before adding it to the recipe.

Weekend Brunch Frittata

3 cloves	garlic, minced (roasting optional, see Step 1)
2 Tbsp (30 mL)	extra virgin olive oil
¼ cup (60 ml)	finely chopped zucchini
¼ cup (60 mL)	finely chopped celery
2	green onions, finely chopped
⅓ cup (80 ml)	finely chopped orange sweet pepper
⅓ cup (80 mL)	finely chopped red sweet pepper
⅓ cup (80 mL)	finely chopped green sweet pepper
⅓ cup (80 mL)	finely chopped yellow sweet pepper
⅓ cup (80 mL)	finely chopped mushrooms
4	omega-3 eggs
¾ cup (185 mL)	cooked red quinoa made with water (see pages 5–6)
½ cup (125 mL)	light ricotta
½ cup (125 mL)	1% cottage cheese
10 oz (300 g)	chopped frozen spinach, thawed and squeezed almost dry
1½ cups (375 mL)	grated extra-old cheddar cheese, divided
1	tomato thinly sliced for garnish

1. Preheat the oven to 350°F (175°C). Lightly grease a 10-inch (25 cm) deep-dish pie plate with canola oil. If roasting garlic, leave whole, wrap in foil and place in oven after it has preheated. Roast until soft, about 20 minutes.

2. In a large non-stick frying pan over medium heat, heat the oil. Add the zucchini, celery, green onions, all four peppers and mushrooms and sauté until translucent and soft, about 4 minutes. If you didn't roast the garlic, add the minced garlic and sauté for 1 minute.

3. Beat the eggs in a large bowl. Stir in the cooked quinoa, ricotta, cottage cheese, sautéed vegetables, spinach and 1 cup (250 mL) of the grated cheddar cheese. If you did roast the garlic add it here and stir in.

4. Pour the mixture into the prepared pie plate.

5. Sprinkle top with the remaining ½ cup (125 mL) of the grated cheese. Place the tomatoes on top of the mixture.

6. Bake in the centre of the oven for 50 to 60 minutes, or until the centre is firm and the edges are golden brown.

7. **TO SERVE:** Remove from the oven and let sit for 10 minutes to cool slightly before cutting into wedges. Serve with a 100% whole grain bread and a mixed green salad if desired.

Makes 1 large frittata • One serving = ⅕ of the frittata

This recipe was originally made by a group of home economists who were at university together 35 years ago and it's been enjoyed at all of their reunions since!

Nutrition per serving

287 calories	19 g total fat	7 g saturated fat
163 mg cholesterol	367 mg sodium	13 g carbohydrates
3 g fibre	4 g sugars	18 g protein

Excellent source of vitamins A and C, folate and calcium.

Serve this protein-rich quiche with a mixed green salad for a great weekend dinner or brunch and get a gold star from the Health Police. NOTE: For convenience, go ahead and use bottled roasted red peppers. Of course, foodies out there: feel free to roast your own. TIP: Instead of fresh baby spinach, you could use about ½ cup (125 mL) of chopped frozen spinach, thawed and drained.

YEAR ROUND

Erin MacGregor, PHEc

Greek-Inspired Quiche

1. Preheat the oven to 400°F (200°C). Lightly spray a 9-inch (23 cm) pie plate with canola oil.

2. **PIE CRUST:** Separate one egg and set aside the egg yolk. Place the egg white in a large bowl. Add the cooked quinoa and Parmesan cheese and mix until well combined.

3. Transfer the quinoa mixture to the prepared pie plate. Using a spatula or your fingers, spread the mixture evenly across the bottom and up the sides of the pie plate to a thickness of about ¼ inch (6 mm).

4. Bake in the centre of the oven for 10 to 12 minutes, until the surface is firm. Remove from the oven.

5. Reduce oven heat to 350°F (175°C).

6. **FILLING:** To a small non-stick frying pan over medium heat, add the oil, onions and garlic and sauté for 2 minutes, or until the onions are translucent. Spoon the mixture into the pie crust and spread evenly.

7. Place the roasted red peppers evenly overtop the mixture on the crust. Then add a layer of spinach.

8. In a medium bowl, whisk together the 5 remaining eggs plus the remaining egg yolk and milk until well incorporated.

9. Pour the egg mixture into the crust and sprinkle the crumbled feta evenly over the surface.

10. Bake in the centre of the oven for 40 to 50 minutes or until the egg mixture has set.

11. **TO SERVE:** Remove from the oven and let sit for 5 minutes before serving. This quiche goes great with a Greek salad.

6	omega-3 eggs, divided (see Step 2)
2 cups (500 mL)	cooked red quinoa, made with water (see pages 5–6)
⅓ cup (80 mL)	finely grated Parmesan cheese
½ tsp (2 mL)	canola oil
½ cup (125 mL)	finely chopped onion
1	clove garlic, minced
½ cup (125 mL)	sliced roasted red pepper (see sidebar)
2 cups (500 mL)	baby spinach
¾ cup (185 mL)	skim milk
¾ cup (185 mL)	crumbled goat feta

Makes one 9-inch (23 cm) quiche • One serving = ⅙ of the quiche

Nutrition per serving

400 calories	14 g total fat	5 g saturated fat
213 mg cholesterol	443 mg sodium	48 g carbohydrates
7 g fibre	6 g sugars	21 g protein

Excellent source of folate, magnesium and zinc.

This pie crust is gluten free, easy to make and tastes great. It can also be used for a fruit filling, which makes it one of those perfect versatile recipes.

Goat Cheese, Red Pepper and Arugula Quiche

PIE CRUST

⅓ cup (80 mL)	quinoa, rinsed and drained
⅔ cup (160 mL)	water
2 Tbsp (30 mL)	non-hydrogenated margarine, melted, divided
3 Tbsp (45 mL)	pasteurized egg whites (see sidebar page 33)
¼ tsp (1 mL)	freshly ground black pepper

FILLING

3½ oz (100 g)	goat feta, cut into small pieces
½ cup (125 mL)	diced red bell pepper
½ cup (125 mL)	tightly packed chopped baby arugula
4	omega-3 eggs
¼ cup (60 mL)	pasteurized egg whites (see sidebar page 33)
¼ cup (60 mL)	water

1. **PIE CRUST:** Place the quinoa in a small saucepan, add the water and bring to a boil. Reduce heat to medium-low and cook covered for 15 to 20 minutes. The quinoa is done when the grains are translucent and all the water has been absorbed. Fluff with a fork, remove from heat and let stand covered for 5 to 10 minutes.

2. Preheat the oven to 400°F (200°C). Lightly brush the inside of a 9-inch (23 cm) pie plate with a little bit of the melted margarine. Reserve the rest and set the pie plate aside.

3. Place the cooked quinoa in a bowl and mash with a spoon.

4. Stir in the egg whites, pepper and the rest of the melted margarine, mixing well. The dough will look pasty; this is a good thing.

5. Transfer the quinoa mixture into the prepared pie plate. Using a spatula or your fingers, spread the mixture evenly across the bottom and three-quarters of the way up the sides of the pie plate to a thickness of about ⅛ inch (3 mm). This is slightly tricky; just do your best.

6. **FILLING:** Place all of the goat cheese, red pepper and arugula into the pie crust.

7. Whisk together the eggs, egg whites and water and then pour this mixture over the cheese and vegetables.

8. Bake in the centre of the oven for 21 to 24 minutes, or until the egg mixture has set.

9. **TO SERVE:** Remove from the oven and let sit for 5 minutes before serving. This quiche goes wonderfully with locally available steamed asparagus.

Makes one 9-inch (23 cm) quiche • One serving = ¼ of the quiche

Nutrition per serving

262 calories	18 g total fat	6 g saturated fat
202 mg cholesterol	254 mg sodium	12 g carbohydrates
2 g fibre	2 g sugars	16 g protein

Excellent source of vitamin B12.

Goat Cheese, Red Pepper and Arugula Quiche

Baked Goodies

CHAPTER SEVEN

Baked Goodies

EVERYBODY NEEDS A TREAT NOW AND THEN. This chapter includes a selection of delicious cookies made with quinoa flour, including two with chocolate chips (perennial favourites), several gluten-free options and even a treat for your four-legged friend. Old-fashioned squares bring up memories of church bazaars, tea parties and our grandmothers. Enter the modern-day quinoa square, which offers more than just calories. The squares in this chapter contain less fat and more fibre and protein than Grandma's but still taste like a hug from the past.

If there are any Cookie Monsters who love chocolate and cranberries living at your house, you might have to hide these morsels before they eat the entire batch. (See photo on page 148.)

Cranberry Chocolate Chip Cookies

1. Preheat the oven to 350°F (175°C). Line a large baking sheet (11- × 17-inch/28 × 42 cm) with parchment paper and set aside.

2. Place the quinoa in a small bowl and add the boiling water. Mix and set aside.

3. In a large bowl, cream together the margarine and sugars until fluffy using either an electric mixer or a wooden spoon. Beat in the eggs one at a time. Add the vanilla and beat in gently.

4. Add the quinoa that has been sitting in the water (including any water that is still there) and beat in gently.

5. In a medium bowl, whisk together the whole wheat and quinoa flours, wheat germ, baking soda and baking powder.

6. Add the flour mixture to the quinoa mixture and beat in gently until well incorporated.

7. Stir in the oats, Bran Buds, flaxseed, chocolate chips and cranberries until well combined.

8. Drop rounded teaspoonfuls of dough onto the prepared baking sheet, leaving at least 2 inches (5 cm) between each spoonful.

9. Bake in the centre of the oven for 12 to 14 minutes, or until golden brown. Remove from the oven and let cool on baking sheet for 1 minute. Transfer from baking sheet and let cool completely on a wire rack. Store in an airtight container in a cool place for up to 1 week or freeze for up to 3 months.

Makes about 56 cookies • One serving = 1 cookie

2 Tbsp (30 mL)	quinoa, rinsed and drained
1 Tbsp (15 mL)	boiling water
1 cup (250 mL)	non-hydrogenated margarine
½ cup (125 mL)	granulated sugar
½ cup (125 mL)	brown sugar, packed
2	omega-3 eggs
1 tsp (5 mL)	pure vanilla extract
1 cup (250 mL)	whole wheat flour
1 cup (250 mL)	quinoa flour (see page 7)
1 Tbsp (15 mL)	wheat germ
1 tsp (5 mL)	baking soda
½ tsp (2 mL)	baking powder
1 cup (250 mL)	large-flake rolled oats
½ cup (125 mL)	Bran Buds™ cereal
¼ cup (60 mL)	ground flaxseed
¾ cup (185 mL)	dark chocolate chips, at least 60% cocoa mass
¾ cup (185 mL)	dried cranberries

Nutrition per serving

93 calories	5 g total fat	1 g saturated fat
7 mg cholesterol	25 mg sodium	12 g carbohydrates
1 g fibre	7 g sugars	1 g protein

Excellent source of vitamin D.

Quinoameal Raisin Cookies (left), Peanut Butter Cookies (middle) (page 151), Cranberry Chocolate Chip Cookies (right) (page 147).

You've heard of oatmeal cookies. Well, this recipe introduces "quinoameal" cookies—yummy treats that are all about quinoa, right down to the flakes. Try adding these to your family's lunch bags. NOTE: Gluten intolerant? Choose a gluten-free baking powder to make these cookies totally gluten free.

YEAR ROUND

Jennifer Hill, PHEc

Quinoameal Raisin Cookies

1. Preheat the oven to 350°F (175°F). Line a large baking sheet (11- × 17-inch/28 × 42 cm) with parchment paper and set aside.

2. In a large bowl, cream together the margarine and sugars. (Use a wooden spoon instead of an electric mixer, as overmixing will result in flat cookies.) Mix in the eggs and vanilla.

3. In a small bowl, combine the quinoa flour, xanthan gum, baking powder and baking soda. Slowly stir the dry ingredients into the margarine mixture until fully combined.

4. Stir in the quinoa flakes and raisins.

5. Drop large spoonfuls of dough (just under the size of a golf ball) onto the prepared baking sheet. You should be able to fit a dozen on a baking sheet.

6. Bake in the centre of the oven for 10 to 15 minutes. For a chewy cookie, bake just until you see the tops turn light brown. For a crispier cookie, bake until the tops are a darker brown. Remove from the oven and let cool on baking sheet for 2 to 3 minutes. Transfer from baking sheet and let cool completely on a wire rack. Store in an airtight container in a cool place for up to 1 week or freeze for up to 3 months.

Makes 42 cookies • One serving = 1 cookie

1 cup (250 mL)	non-hydrogenated margarine
½ cup (125 mL)	granulated sugar
1 cup (250 mL)	brown sugar, packed
2	omega-3 eggs, beaten
½ tsp (2 mL)	pure vanilla extract
2 cups (500 mL)	quinoa flour (see page 7)
1 tsp (5 mL)	xanthan gum (see sidebar page 35)
1 tsp (5 mL)	baking powder (see Note in recipe introduction)
1 tsp (5 mL)	baking soda
2½ cups (625 mL)	quinoa flakes (see page 7)
1 cup (250 mL)	sultana raisins

When baking use pure vanilla extract to add the best possible flavour.

Nutrition per serving

128 calories	6 g total fat	1 g saturated fat
0 mg cholesterol	36 mg sodium	18 g carbohydrates
1 g fibre	10 g sugars	2 g protein

Excellent source of vitamin D.

This gingersnap gets its flavour from both dried and fresh ginger. Their spicy taste makes these cookies great for Christmas or holiday baking. They are delicious and also happen to be gluten free. NOTE: To add some glam, drizzle finished cookies with melted dark chocolate, let set and serve.

Gingersnaps

½ cup (125 mL)   canola oil

1 cup (250 mL)   granulated sugar

¼ cup (60 mL)   molasses

1   omega-3 egg

1 cup + 2 Tbsp   quinoa flour (see page 7)
(280 mL)

¾ cup (185 mL)   brown rice flour

1 tsp (5 mL)   baking soda

2 tsp (10 mL)   ground ginger

1 Tbsp (15 mL)   cinnamon

2 Tbsp (30 mL)   finely grated fresh ginger

1. Preheat the oven to 375°F (190°C). Line a large baking sheet (11- × 17-inch/28 × 42 cm) with parchment paper and set aside.

2. In a large mixing bowl, beat together the oil and sugar using either an electric mixer or a wooden spoon.

3. Add the molasses and egg. Beat until fluffy. This takes 2 to 3 minutes with a mixer and about 5 minutes with a wooden spoon.

4. Stir in the quinoa and brown rice flours, baking soda, ground ginger, cinnamon and fresh ginger until the dough comes together.

5. Scoop teaspoonfuls of dough onto the prepared baking sheet fitting 12 per cookie sheet. For picture-perfect cookies, try using a mini scoop for the dough.

6. Bake in the centre of the oven for 12 to 14 minutes, or until golden brown. For a chewy cookie, bake for 12 minutes; for a crispy one, bake for 14 minutes.

7. Remove from the oven and let cool on baking sheet for 1 minute. Transfer from baking sheet and let cool completely on a wire rack. Store in an airtight container in a cool place for up to 1 week or freeze for up to 3 months.

Makes 40 cookies • One serving = 2 cookies

Nutrition per serving

152 calories	6 g total fat	0 g saturated fat
10 mg cholesterol	48 mg sodium	23 g carbohydrates
1 g fibre	12 g sugars	2 g protein

Excellent source of vitamin D.

A simple spin on a popular recipe and supplying 6 grams of protein per serving (that's two cookies), this is a great choice as an after-school snack for kids and teens. (See photo on page 148.) NOTE: Chocolate lover? You can always add ½ cup (125 mL) of chocolate chunks or chips to the dough.

YEAR ROUND

Janet Butters, PHEc

Peanut Butter Cookies

1 cup (250 mL)	crunchy peanut butter
½ cup (125 mL)	brown sugar, packed
1	omega-3 egg
½ tsp (2 mL)	pure vanilla extract
½ cup (125 mL)	quinoa flour (see page 7)

1. Preheat the oven to 350°F (175°C). Line a large baking sheet (11- × 17-inch/28 × 42 cm) with parchment paper and set aside.

2. In a medium bowl, mix together the peanut butter and sugar using a wooden spoon.

3. In a small bowl, beat together the egg and vanilla. Stir this into the peanut butter mixture.

4. Add the quinoa flour and stir until all combined.

5. Shape the dough into 28 equal-sized balls, using about 1 tsp (5 mL) of dough for each. Place balls on the prepared baking sheet, leaving at least 2 inches (5 cm) between each ball. With a moistened fork, make a grid pattern on top of each, flattening each ball into a 2½-inch (6 cm) cookie.

6. Bake in the centre of the oven for 13 to 15 minutes. Remove from the oven and let cool on baking sheet at least 10 minutes. Transfer from baking sheet and let cool completely on a wire rack. Store in an airtight container in a cool place for up to 5 days.

Makes 28 cookies • One serving = 2 cookies

Nutrition per serving

161 calories	10 g total fat	2 g saturated fat
14 mg cholesterol	82 mg sodium	15 g carbohydrates
2 g fibre	9 g sugars	6 g protein

YEAR ROUND

Mairlyn Smith, PHEc

Hands up, who doesn't love chocolate chip cookies? Okay, all five of you turn to page 149 and make the Quinoameal Raisin Cookies. Everybody else, get out your bowls. The added wheat germ makes this a whole-grain cookie.

Chocolate Chip Cookies

½ cup (125 mL)	unsalted non-hydrogenated margarine
½ cup (125 mL)	brown sugar, packed
¼ cup (60 mL)	granulated sugar
1	omega-3 egg
1 tsp (5 mL)	pure vanilla extract
¾ cup (185 mL)	quinoa flour (see page 7)
½ cup (125 mL)	whole wheat flour
2 Tbsp (30 mL)	wheat germ
½ tsp (2 mL)	baking soda
¼ cup (60 mL)	dark chocolate chips, at least 60% cocoa mass

1. Preheat the oven to 375°F (190°C). Line a large baking sheet (11- × 17-inch/28 × 42 cm) with parchment paper and set aside.

2. In a medium bowl, cream together the margarine and sugars until fluffy using either an electric mixer or a wooden spoon. Add the egg and vanilla, beating until fluffy.

3. Stir in the quinoa and whole wheat flours, wheat germ, baking soda and chocolate chips.

4. Drop rounded teaspoonfuls of dough onto the prepared baking sheet or use a mini scoop.

5. Bake in the centre of the oven for 10 to 12 minutes. These cookies are chewy when baked for 11 minutes and start to get really crispy after 12 minutes—your choice. Remove from the oven and let cool slightly on baking sheet. Transfer from baking sheet and let cool completely on a wire rack. Store in an airtight container in a cool place for up to 1 week or freeze for up to 2 months.

Makes 40 cookies • 1 serving = 2 cookies

Nutrition per serving

124 calories	6 g total fat	1 g saturated fat
10 mg cholesterol	27 mg sodium	15 g carbohydrates
1 g fibre	9 g sugars	2 g protein

Totally gluten-free, these cookies require sorghum flour, which is available at either a health food store or a bulk store. You'll enjoy the crunch of these delightful cookies. Go ahead, try to eat just one!

YEAR ROUND

Donna Washburn, PHEc,
& Heather Butt, PHEc

Gluten-Free Quinoa Flax Cookies

1. Preheat the oven to 350°F (175°C). Line a large baking sheet (11- × 17-inch/28 × 42 cm) with parchment paper and set aside.

2. In a medium bowl combine the sorghum and quinoa flours, ground flaxseed, cracked flaxseed, baking soda and xanthan gum. Mix well and set aside.

3. In a large bowl, using a handheld electric mixer on low speed, cream the margarine and sugars until combined. Beat in the egg yolk and vanilla until light and fluffy. Slowly beat in the dry ingredients until combined. Stir in the quinoa flakes.

4. Shape the dough into 1-inch (2.5 cm) balls. Place on the prepared baking sheet, leaving at least 2 inches (5 cm) between each ball. Flatten each ball with the bottom of a moistened drinking glass. The thinner they are pressed, the crispier the cookies will be.

5. Bake in the centre of the oven for 10 to 15 minutes, or until set. Remove from the oven and let cool on baking sheet for 2 minutes. Transfer from baking sheet and let cool completely on a wire rack. Store in an airtight container at room temperature for up to 2 weeks or in the freezer for up to 2 months.

Makes 18 cookies • One serving = 1 cookie

¼ cup (60 mL)	sorghum flour
¼ cup (60 mL)	quinoa flour (see page 7)
2 Tbsp (30 mL)	ground flaxseed
⅓ cup (80 mL)	flaxseed, cracked or lightly ground
1 tsp (5 mL)	baking soda
1 tsp (5 mL)	xanthan gum (see sidebar page 35)
¼ cup (60 mL)	non-hydrogenated margarine
¼ cup (60 mL)	brown sugar, packed
2 Tbsp (30 mL)	granulated sugar
1	omega-3 egg yolk
½ tsp (2 mL)	pure vanilla extract
⅓ cup (80 mL)	quinoa flakes (see page 7)

Flaxseeds contain plant lignins that have been shown to be potent cancer fighters. Flaxseeds also contain heart-healthy omega-3 fatty acids and two types of fibre—one to keep your colon happy and the other to help lower your cholesterol.

Nutrition per serving

77 calories	4 g total fat	1 g saturated fat
11 mg cholesterol	52 mg sodium	9 g carbohydrates
1 g fibre	4 g sugars	1 g protein

What are brownies doing in the cookie section? These ones are small, bite-sized and loaded with the yum factor—everything a cookie should be. NOTE: For an extra-special treat, press a chocolate macaroon or mini Rolo chocolate treat into the centre of each Brownie Bite before baking. Calories? They go way up, but for a special treat, that's okay, once in a while . . .

Brownie Bites

½ cup (125 mL)	quinoa flour (see page 7)
⅓ cup (80 mL)	natural cocoa powder, sifted if lumpy (see sidebar)
1 tsp (5 mL)	baking powder
2	omega-3 eggs
⅔ cup (160 mL)	granulated sugar
⅓ cup (80 mL)	canola oil
1 tsp (5 mL)	pure vanilla extract

Natural cocoa powder contains higher levels of heart-healthy flavanols. Hershey's natural and Ghiradelli natural are both available in Canada in larger grocery stores.

1. Preheat the oven to 325°F (160°C). Lightly spray 24 mini muffin cups with canola oil.

2. In a small bowl, whisk together the quinoa flour, cocoa powder and baking powder until well mixed.

3. In a large bowl, whisk together the eggs, sugar, oil and vanilla until blended.

4. Add the flour mixture to the egg mixture, whisking until blended.

5. Divide the batter between the muffin cups, filling each with about 1 Tbsp (15 mL) of batter. The cups should be about two-thirds full.

6. Bake in the centre of the oven for 13 to 15 minutes, until the brownies are slightly puffed and a toothpick inserted into one comes out with a few crumbs clinging to it. Don't overbake.

7. Remove from the oven and let cool in pan on a wire rack for 2 minutes, then turn the pan over. After a minute or two, lift up the pan. Brownie Bites should have released from the pan onto the rack. Carefully turn each brownie over to finish cooling on rack.

8. TO SERVE: For a simple yet delicious dessert, plate brownies and sprinkle with icing sugars and cocoa powder or serve on a puddle of raspberry coulis (see photo).

Make 24 mini muffin–size brownies • One serving = 3 brownies

Nutrition per serving

202 calories	12 g total fat	0 g saturated fat
48 mg cholesterol	17 mg sodium	24 g carbohydrates
2 g fibre	17 g sugars	3 g protein

Brownie Bites

"They're not too sweet, they're not too chocolatey," according to Goldilocks. "Yes, these treats are just right!"

Chocolatey Banana Squares

BASE

¾ cup (185 mL)	large-flake rolled oats
2 Tbsp (30 mL)	quinoa flour (see page 7)
¼ cup (60 mL)	whole wheat flour
¼ cup (60 mL)	dark brown sugar, packed
½ tsp (2 mL)	baking powder
3 Tbsp (45 mL)	non-hydrogenated margarine, melted
1½ Tbsp (22 mL)	skim milk
1 cup (250 mL)	cooked quinoa, made with water (see pages 5–6)

TOPPING

¼ cup (60 mL)	quinoa flour (see page 7)
2 Tbsp (30 mL)	whole wheat flour
¼ tsp (1 mL)	baking powder
1	omega-3 egg
¾ cup (185 mL)	granulated sugar
1 tsp (5 mL)	pure vanilla extract
½ cup (125 mL)	mashed banana (about 1 large, very ripe)
3 Tbsp (45 mL)	non-hydrogenated margarine, melted
6 Tbsp (90 mL)	natural cocoa powder, sifted if lumpy (see sidebar page 154)

1. Preheat the oven to 375°F (190°C). Lightly grease an 8-inch (20 cm) square metal baking pan with canola oil.

2. **BASE:** In a medium bowl, stir together the rolled oats, quinoa and whole wheat flours, brown sugar and baking powder. Pour in the melted margarine and stir to coat the dry ingredients. Mix in the cooked quinoa and then stir in the milk to moisten. The mixture will be crumbly. Using your hands or a spatula, press the mixture evenly into the prepared baking pan.

3. **TOPPING:** In a small bowl, combine the quinoa and whole wheat flours and baking powder.

4. In a medium bowl, beat together the egg, sugar, vanilla and mashed banana with a whisk or electric mixer until well blended. Pour in the melted margarine and beat until smooth.

5. Gradually add the cocoa powder, whisking in slowly to begin. Continue to whisk until the cocoa powder is fully incorporated. Stir in the flour mixture just until combined. Spread evenly over the prepared quinoa base.

6. Bake in the centre of the oven for 30 to 35 minutes, or until a toothpick inserted in the centre of the pan comes out with a few moist crumbs clinging to it. Remove from the oven and let cool in pan on a wire rack for about 30 minutes before cutting into bars. Store in an airtight container in a cool place for up to 1 week.

Makes 16 squares • One serving = 1 square

Nutrition per serving

147 calories	6 g total fat	1 g saturated fat
12 mg cholesterol	15 mg sodium	23 g carbohydrates
2 g fibre	14 g sugars	2 g protein

Excellent source of vitamin D.

The chia seeds are another South American food that's joined the ranks of the superfoods. High in omega-3 fatty acids and fibre, chia seeds help slow down the rate at which your body breaks down carbohydrates. They're the hidden crunch factor in this chocolatey cookie. You can find chia seeds in larger grocery stores that have a health food section.

YEAR ROUND

Mairlyn Smith, PHEc

Chocolate Chia Cookies

½ cup (125 mL)	non-hydrogenated margarine
¼ cup (60 mL)	black chia seeds
1 cup (250 mL)	dark brown sugar, packed
¼ cup (60 mL)	liquid honey
1	omega-3 egg
½ cup (125 mL)	natural cocoa powder (see sidebar page 154)
1 cup (250 mL)	quinoa flour (see page 7)
¾ cup (185 mL)	quinoa flakes (see page 7)
1 tsp (5 mL)	cinnamon
1 tsp (5 mL)	baking soda
¼ cup (60 mL)	dark chocolate chips, at least 60% cocoa mass

1. Preheat the oven to 375°F (190°C). Line a large baking sheet (11- × 17-inch/28 × 42 cm) with parchment paper and set aside.

2. In a medium bowl, cream the margarine using either an electric mixer or a wooden spoon. Beat in the chia seeds. Add the brown sugar and honey and beat until fluffy.

3. Add the egg and beat until cream coloured.

4. Gently stir in the cocoa powder, then beat until well incorporated.

5. Gently stir in the quinoa flour, quinoa flakes, cinnamon and baking soda until there is no visible flour. Stir in the chocolate chips until well distributed.

6. Drop by rounded teaspoonful or mini-scoop onto the baking sheet.

7. Bake in the centre of the oven for 12 to 14 minutes. Let cool for at least 5 minutes before removing from the baking sheet. Finish cooling on a wire cooling rack. Store in an airtight container for up to 1 week or freeze for up to 2 months.

Makes 48 cookies • One serving = 1 cookie

Nutrition per serving

94 calories	4 g total fat	1 g saturated fat
5 mg cholesterol	26 mg sodium	13 g carbohydrates
1 g fibre	8 g sugars	1 g protein

Apple Carrot
Doggie Biscotti

Quinoa is for everyone, including your pet. And your pet deserves a treat too! These doggie treats are wheat free for all those sensitive pooches out there. NOTE: If you don't have a food processor, use a blender. Add the water, honey and oil with the apples and carrots to help the blender purée more easily, then add the flaxseed and pulse until incorporated.

YEAR ROUND

Jennifer MacKenzie,
PHEc

Apple Carrot Doggie Biscotti

1. Preheat the oven to 350°F (175°C). Line 2 large baking sheets (11- × 17-inch/28 × 42 cm) with parchment paper or foil sprayed with canola oil.

2. In a large bowl, whisk together the quinoa and brown rice flours, potato starch, cinnamon, baking powder and baking soda. Set aside.

3. In a food processor, pulse the apples and carrots until finely chopped. Add the flaxseed, water, honey and oil and process until fairly smooth. Pour over the dry ingredients and, using a wooden spoon, stir until evenly moistened.

4. Divide the dough in half. Dust your work surface and hands with rice flour and shape each half into a log about 15 inches (38 cm) long for small biscotti or 8 inches (20 cm) long for large biscotti. Place the logs at least 3 inches (8 cm) apart on the prepared baking sheets.

5. Lightly press logs down with your hands to flatten until they are 2 inches (5 cm) wide for small biscotti or 3½ inches (9 cm) wide for large biscotti. Prick the logs all over with a fork.

6. Bake in the centre of the oven for about 40 minutes, or until a cake tester or toothpick inserted in the centre comes out clean. Remove from the oven and set the baking sheets to cool on a wire rack for 10 minutes. Reduce oven heat to 300°F (150°C).

7. Cut the logs crosswise into slices about ¼ inch (6 mm) thick. Place the slices cut side down on the baking sheets. Bake for another 20 minutes at 300°F (150°C). Flip biscotti over and bake for about 20 minutes, or until dry and crisp. Turn off oven, leaving biscotti in, and let cool completely. Store cooled doggie biscotti in a cookie tin or glass jar at room temperature for up to 1 month.

2 cups (500 mL)	quinoa flour (see page 7)
1½ cups (375 mL)	brown rice flour
⅓ cup (80 mL)	potato starch
1 tsp (5 mL)	ground cinnamon
½ tsp (2 mL)	baking powder
¼ tsp (1 mL)	baking soda
1½ cups (375 mL)	cored and chopped apples
1 cup (250 mL)	carrots, scrubbed well and coarsely chopped
¼ cup (60 mL)	ground flaxseed
¼ cup (60 mL)	water
¼ cup (60 mL)	liquid honey
2 Tbsp (30 mL)	canola oil

Makes about 100 small biscotti or 60 large biscotti • One serving = 1 large biscotti

Nutrition per serving

47 calories	1 g total fat	0 g saturated fat
0 mg cholesterol	12 mg sodium	9 g carbohydrates
1 g fibre	2 g sugars	1 g protein

This great little square can be served as dessert or a snack cake; it's also just right for after school. Okay, it's great any time of the day . . .

Chocolate Chip Squares

1 cup (250 mL)	quinoa flour (see page 7)
¾ cup (185 mL)	wheat germ
¼ tsp (2 mL)	cinnamon
¼ cup (60 mL)	dark chocolate chips, at least 60% cocoa mass
1	medium banana, very ripe, mashed
¾ cup (185 mL)	brown sugar, packed
½ cup (125 mL)	canola oil
½ cup (125 mL)	liquid honey
2 Tbsp (30 mL)	peanut butter
1	omega-3 egg
2 tsp (10 mL)	pure vanilla extract
1½ cups (375 mL)	cooked quinoa made with water (see pages 5–6)

1. Preheat the oven to 350°F (175°C). Lightly grease a 9- × 13-inch (3.5 L) metal baking pan with canola oil.

2. In a large bowl, mix together the quinoa flour, wheat germ, cinnamon and chocolate chips. Set aside.

3. In another large bowl, gently beat together the mashed banana, brown sugar, oil, honey, peanut butter, egg and vanilla. Add this to the dry ingredients. Mix together until well combined.

4. Fold in the cooked quinoa until well distributed. Pour into the prepared pan, using a spatula to scrape out all the batter from the sides of the bowl. Smooth out the top of the batter in the pan. Bake for 30 to 35 minutes, or until a toothpick inserted in the centre comes out clean.

5. Cool in the pan on a wire rack for 5 minutes. Remove from the pan by carefully flipping over onto the wire rack. Cool completely, then flip back onto a cutting board. Cut into 20 squares and store in an airtight container in a cool place for up to 3 days.

Makes 20 squares • One serving = 1 square

Nutrition per serving

179 calories	8 g total fat	1 g saturated fat
10 mg cholesterol	13 mg sodium	25 g carbohydrates
2 g fibre	17 g sugars	3 g protein

Heart-healthy ground walnuts and quinoa flakes plus the sweetness of dates make these simple vegan squares a treat you'll want to make often. NOTE: Use a food processor to grind the walnuts for this recipe.

YEAR ROUND

Nazima Qureshi, OHEA
student member

Date and Walnut Squares

1. Preheat the oven to 350°F (175°C). Lightly spray an 8-inch (20 cm) square metal baking pan with canola oil.

2. In a medium saucepan, add the dates, orange juice, water and margarine. Heat over medium heat for 10 minutes, stirring occasionally. Stir in the orange zest and remove from heat.

3. In a medium bowl, mix together the quinoa flakes, ground nuts and cinnamon.

4. Add the dry mixture to the date mixture, using a large spoon, and stir until well incorporated.

5. Spoon the mixture into the prepared pan and press down with the back of the spoon. Bake in the centre of the oven for 15 minutes. The squares will be very dense and fruity. Remove from the oven and let cool in the pan for 20 minutes. Cut into 16 squares and let cool completely in the pan on a wire rack before serving. Store in an airtight container in a cool place for up to 3 days.

Makes 16 squares • One serving = 1 square

1 lb (500 g)	dried pitted dates (see page 25)
½ cup (125 mL)	fresh orange juice
1 cup (250 mL)	water
2 tsp (10 mL)	non-hydrogenated margarine
Zest of 1	orange
1 cup (250 mL)	quinoa flakes (see page 7)
1½ cups (375 mL)	walnut halves, ground
1½ tsp (7 mL)	cinnamon

Nutrition per serving

187 calories	8 g total fat	1 g saturated fat
0 mg cholesterol	3 mg sodium	30 g carbohydrates
4 g fibre	21 g sugars	3 g protein

YEAR ROUND

Andrea Villneff, OHEA
provisional member

Brownies are a must in any cookbook worth its weight in chocolate, but healthy alternatives are always a challenge in the treat department. Enter Chocolate Black-Bean Brownies—a healthier twist on a classic favourite using heart-healthy natural cocoa powder and protein-rich black beans. Yes, black beans! Sshhh, don't tell, and no one will ever know.

Chocolate Black-Bean Brownies

1 can (19 oz/540 mL)	black beans, rinsed and drained
1 cup (250 mL)	water
1 tsp (5 mL)	pure vanilla extract
2 cups (500 mL)	brown sugar, packed
1½ cups (375 mL)	quinoa flour (see page 7)
1¼ cups (310 mL)	natural cocoa, sifted if lumpy (see sidebar page 154)
1 cup (250 mL)	coarsely chopped walnuts (optional)
1 tsp (5 mL)	baking powder
1½ cups (375 mL)	cooked quinoa made with water (see pages 5–6)

For easier slicing, use a knife dipped in hot water and wiped clean.

1. Preheat the oven to 350°F (175°C). Lightly grease a 9- × 13-inch (3.5 L) metal baking pan with canola oil.

2. In a food processor, pulse the beans. Slowly add the water to purée. Add the vanilla and pulse once or twice to combine. Set aside.

3. In a large bowl, mix together the brown sugar, quinoa flour, cocoa, walnuts (if using) and baking powder. Gently fold in the cooked quinoa.

4. Add the bean purée mixture. Stir well to combine. The batter will be very thick.

5. Spoon the batter into the prepared pan. Flatten the top with a spoon or spatula. Bake in the centre of the oven for 50 to 55 minutes, or until the centre is firm and a toothpick comes out clean. Remove from the oven and cool completely on a wire rack before cutting. Carefully cut exactly 16 squares (see sidebar) and store in a covered container in a cool place for up to 4 days.

Makes 16 brownies • One serving = 1 brownie (without nuts)

Nutrition per serving

219 calories	2 g total fat	0 g saturated fat
0 mg cholesterol	16 mg sodium	46 g carbohydrates
4 g fibre	27 g sugars	5 g protein

CHAPTER EIGHT

Desserts

Desserts

SOMETIMES AN OCCASION CALLS FOR A SIMPLE ENDING, sometimes it calls for a big bang and sometimes it calls for an elegant morsel. Take your pick from the desserts in this chapter.

Move over, rice pudding. We begin with a selection of scrumptious quinoa puddings. What is it about warm pudding that makes it such a comfort food? Is it the creamy consistency, the subtle sweetness or the fact that on a cold fall or winter evening, you just want something warm and slightly sweet as a treat? Whatever the reason, here are several cool-weather recipes and one summer version, just to break the rules, that answer the call for "Pudding, please!"

Rounding out the chapter—and the recipes in this book—are a handful of other desserts that range from fruity to nutty and, of course, include some dark chocolate, just for good measure. Where would a special occasion be without it?

This pudding combines pure maple syrup and tart cherries, giving this dessert a decadent flavour that will warm your heart and your soul.

FALL and **WINTER**

Jennifer MacKenzie, PHEc

Maple Cherry Pudding

1. Place the quinoa flour in a deep medium saucepan and gradually whisk in the milk until mixture is smooth. Whisk in the water, maple syrup and quinoa. Bring to a simmer over medium-high heat, uncovered, whisking often to prevent scorching.

2. Reduce heat to low, cover and simmer, stirring occasionally, for 20 minutes, or until quinoa is tender.

3. Increase heat to medium-low, stir in the cherries and cook uncovered, stirring often, for about 5 minutes, or until quinoa is very soft, cherries are plump and pudding is slightly thickened. It will thicken further upon cooling.

4. **TO SERVE:** Remove from heat and stir in the vanilla. Let cool slightly and serve warm.

Makes 2½ cups (625 mL) • **One serving = about ⅔ cup (160 mL)**

2 Tbsp (30 mL)	quinoa flour (see page 7)
1½ cups (375 mL)	1% milk
1 cup (250 mL)	water
2 Tbsp (30 mL)	pure maple syrup
⅓ cup (80 mL)	quinoa, rinsed and drained
¼ cup (60 mL)	dried sour (tart) cherries
½ tsp (2 mL)	pure vanilla extract

Nutrition per serving

167 calories	2 g total fat	1 g saturated fat
4 mg cholesterol	59 mg sodium	30 g carbohydrates
2 g fibre	11 g sugars	6 g protein

This dessert tastes like a coconut macaroon but has the consistency of a very soft, creamy rice pudding. If you love chocolate and coconut, this one has your name on it.

FALL and **WINTER**

Heike Beatrix Heinze, PHEc

Chocolate Macaroon Pudding

½ cup (125 mL)	quinoa, rinsed and drained
1 can (14 oz/398 mL)	light coconut milk
1 cup (250 mL)	water
½ cup (125 mL)	liquid honey
¼ cup (60 mL)	natural cocoa powder, sifted if lumpy (see sidebar page 154)
1 Tbsp (15 mL)	coconut extract
¼ cup (60 mL)	unsweetened shredded coconut, medium

1. Place the quinoa in a medium saucepan, add the coconut milk and water and bring to a boil. Reduce heat to medium-low and cook covered for 20 minutes, or until the quinoa is tender. Remove lid, stir and let simmer uncovered for 10 to 15 minutes, or until the pudding has become thicker.

2. Remove from heat, stir and let stand for 5 minutes.

3. Meanwhile, in a small bowl, whisk together the honey, cocoa powder and coconut extract until smooth.

4. Whisk the honey mixture into the quinoa mixture. Add the coconut and stir well.

5. **TO SERVE:** Cool slightly and either spoon into five small dessert bowls or into a medium bowl and refrigerate until serving time. To take an everyday dessert and make it glamorous, serve this pudding in elegant glasses and garnish with chocolate shavings (see photo).

Makes 2½ cups (625 mL) • **One serving = ½ cup (125 mL)**

Nutrition per serving

275 calories	9 g total fat	6 g saturated fat
0 mg cholesterol	37 mg sodium	46 g carbohydrates
3 g fibre	32 g sugars	3 g protein

Here's a warm dessert that offers the health goodness of apricots and blueberries with a touch of coconut. Advice for the coconut fans in the crowd: for a more intense flavour, use coconut extract.

Coconut Parfait with Apricots and Blueberries

½ cup (125 mL)	quinoa, rinsed and drained
¾ cup (185 mL)	canned light coconut milk
¼ cup (60 mL)	water
1 tsp (5 mL)	coconut or almond extract
⅓ cup (80 mL)	fresh or dried blueberries
⅓ cup (80 mL)	fresh or dried apricots, sliced
2 tsp (10 mL)	pure maple syrup
4 tsp (20 mL)	coarsely chopped whole almonds

1. In a medium saucepan over medium heat, bring the quinoa, coconut milk, water and extract of your choice to a boil. Cover and cook for 12 to 15 minutes, until the quinoa has absorbed most of the liquid. Fluff with a fork, remove from heat and let stand covered for 15 minutes. Remove lid to let cool slightly.

2. **TO ASSEMBLE:** In 4 parfait glasses, wine glasses or clear glass dessert bowls, layer the quinoa and the fruit, starting with the quinoa and finishing with quinoa.

3. **TO SERVE:** Top each parfait with ½ tsp (2 mL) maple syrup and 1 tsp (5 mL) almonds.

Makes 2 cups (500 mL) • One serving = ½ cup (125 mL)

Nutrition per serving

152 calories	6 g total fat	2 g saturated fat
0 mg cholesterol	14 mg sodium	21 g carbohydrates
2 g fibre	5 g sugars	4 g protein

A twist on traditional baked rice pudding, this recipe is cooked in the oven using a *bain-marie*, a water bath that prevents the pudding from burning. You will need a large shallow roasting pan as well as an 8-inch (20 cm) square baking dish. Apples recommended for this recipe are Gala, Cortland or McIntosh.

FALL and **WINTER**

Janet Butters, PHEc

Baked Pudding

1. Place the quinoa in a large saucepan, add 2 cups (500 mL) of the milk and bring to a boil. Reduce heat to medium-low and cook covered for 18 to 20 minutes, stirring occasionally. Remove from heat. Remove lid and let cool.

2. When the quinoa is cool to the touch, preheat the oven to 325°F (160°C). Lightly grease an 8-inch (20 cm) square baking dish with canola oil.

3. Boil about 8 cups (2 L) of water. You will need this for the hot-water bath (*bain-marie*) the pudding is going to be cooking in.

4. In a small bowl, mix together the raisins, lemon zest and flour. Set aside.

5. Combine the remaining ½ cup (125 mL) of milk, sugar, margarine, vanilla and eggs and beat well using a wire whisk. Mix into the cooled quinoa.

6. In a large bowl, toss the apple slices with the cinnamon. Place one-third of the apples in the bottom of the prepared pan in a single layer.

7. Pour half of the quinoa mixture over top. Lay the next third of the apple slices on top of the quinoa. Repeat with the quinoa and top with the remaining apple slices.

8. Place the baking dish in the roasting pan. Carefully pour the boiling water into the roasting pan until it comes halfway up the outside of the baking dish.

9. Bake in the centre of the oven for 1 hour.

10. **TO SERVE:** Remove from the oven, remove baking dish from the *bain-marie* and let set for 10 minutes. Serve warm, either plain or with a splash of maple syrup.

Makes 6 cups (1.5 L) • **One serving = 1 cup (250 mL)**

1 cup (250 mL)	quinoa, rinsed and drained
2½ cups (625 mL)	1% milk, divided
⅓ cup (80 mL)	raisins
½ tsp (2 mL)	lemon zest
1 Tbsp (15 mL)	quinoa flour (see page 7)
2½ Tbsp (37 mL)	brown sugar, packed
1½ tsp (7 mL)	melted non-hydrogenated margarine
½ tsp (2 mL)	pure vanilla extract
3	omega-3 eggs
6	apples, peeled, cored and thinly sliced
1 Tbsp (15 mL)	cinnamon
	Pure maple syrup for serving (optional)

Although this recipe may sound and smell like a dessert, it contains enough protein to put it in either the breakfast or lunch category. Not that hungry? Halve the serving size.

Nutrition per serving

307 calories	6 g total fat	2 g saturated fat
99 mg cholesterol	94 mg sodium	55 g carbohydrates
5 g fibre	23 g sugars	12 g protein

Custards need to be baked in a *bain-marie*. What's a *bain-marie*, you ask? See page 169 for the answer to this culinary cooking method. NOTE: To change up this recipe, add ¼ cup (60 mL) of raisins with the quinoa and substitute ground cinnamon for the nutmeg.

Baked Custard

¼ cup (60 mL)	quinoa, rinsed and drained
¾ cup (185 mL)	water
1	omega-3 egg
1 cup (250 mL)	skim or 1% milk
¼ cup (60 mL)	brown sugar, packed
½ tsp (2 mL)	ground nutmeg

To safely remove ramekins from the boiling water, slide a spatula under each. Lift gently and, once clear of the water, support the ramekin with an oven-mitt-covered hand while transferring it to the rack.

1. Place the quinoa in a small saucepan, add the water and bring to a boil. Reduce heat to medium-low and cook covered for 18 to 20 minutes. The quinoa is done when the grains are translucent and all the water has been absorbed. Fluff with a fork, remove from heat and let stand covered for 5 to 10 minutes.

2. Preheat the oven to 350°F (175°C). Lightly grease two ¾-cup (185 mL) ramekins with canola oil.

3. Boil about 4 cups (1 L) of water. You will need this for the hot-water bath (*bain-marie*) the custard is going to be cooking in.

4. In a medium bowl, whisk together the egg and milk. Stir in the cooked quinoa, brown sugar and nutmeg until blended. Pour mixture into the prepared ramekins.

5. Place the ramekins in a 9-inch (23 cm) square baking pan. Pour enough boiling water into the baking pan to reach halfway up the sides of the ramekins.

6. Bake in the centre of the oven for 30 minutes, or until a cake tester inserted in the centre comes out clean.

7. **TO SERVE:** Carefully remove the ramekins from the hot water (see sidebar) and let cool on a wire rack for 30 minutes. Serve warm. These custards can also be covered and refrigerated for up to 3 days and served cold.

Makes about 1 cup (250 mL) • One serving = ½ cup (125 mL)

Nutrition per serving

263 calories	4 g total fat	1 g saturated fat
97 mg cholesterol	96 mg sodium	47 g carbohydrates
1 g fibre	33 g sugars	10 g protein

Excellent source of riboflavin, vitamins B12 and D.

Everything old becomes new again. Crêpes were all the rage in the 1970s and are now making a comeback. This recipe will give you a slightly sweet basic crêpe that you can use in recipes with fruit or sweeter sauces, such as the Autumn Apple Crêpes (page 172).

YEAR ROUND

Deb Campbell, PHEc

Basic Quinoa Crêpes

1. In a food processor fitted with a metal blade, process the flour, eggs, oil and soy beverage for 10 to 15 seconds, until smooth (batter must be lump free). Refrigerate batter for at least 30 minutes before cooking. This allows bubbles to dissipate and gives a nicer finished product.

2. Very lightly grease a small frying pan (7-inch/18 cm) with canola oil. You may only have to do this once; a lightly seasoned pan will give you a more uniform crêpe pancake (see sidebar).

3. Spoon a scant 3 Tbsp (45 mL) of the batter into the pan and rotate the pan around so that there is an even coating on the bottom of it. Try not to run batter up the sides as this will overcrisp the edges. Turn the crêpe over after 30 seconds. Crêpe will be lightly browned on both sides and will be flexible (for folding or rolling).

4. Place the cooked crêpes on a plate lined with parchment paper to cool. They can either be used in other crêpe recipes or can be frozen at this point for later use. Freeze in small amounts, placing a small piece of parchment between the crêpes and wrapping them in clear plastic wrap. Freeze for up to 1 month.

Makes 12 crêpes • One serving = 1 crêpe

¾ cup (185 mL)	quinoa flour (see page 7)
3	omega-3 eggs
¼ cup (60 mL)	canola oil
1 cup (250 mL)	organic vanilla soy beverage

Tips for making perfect crêpes

A crêpe pan helps. If you don't have one, use a heavy-bottomed non-stick frying pan.

To measure 3 Tbsp (45 mL) of batter for a single crêpe, use a ¼ cup (60 mL) measuring cup filled three-quarters full.

It's all in the wrist! As you add the crêpe batter to the pan, swirl the pan at the same time— sort of like patting your head and rubbing your stomach at the same time.

The oil helps. Make sure you either use a well-seasoned pan or lightly brush the pan before making each crêpe.

Never use soap on a well-seasoned pan. Instead, wipe it clean with a paper towel.

Nutrition per serving

84 calories	6 g total fat	1 g saturated fat
16 mg cholesterol	15 mg sodium	6 g carbohydrates
1 g fibre	1 g sugars	2 g protein

In Canada we know how to grow apples. With the huge variety available in the fall and winter months, stretch out your culinary tastes and experiment with different varieties (see sidebar).
NOTE: For this recipe we used Astro Original French Vanilla Yogurt, with 1.5 grams total fat per ½ cup (125 mL), for its flavour and lower fat content.

Autumn Apple Crêpes

1 recipe	Basic Quinoa Crêpes (page 171)
2 Tbsp (30 mL)	non-hydrogenated margarine
4	apples, peeled and thinly sliced (see sidebar)
½ cup (125 mL)	brown sugar, packed
½ tsp (2 mL)	cinnamon + some for garnish
¼ tsp (1 mL)	nutmeg
1½ cups (375 mL)	Astro Original French Vanilla Yogurt or a similar fat-reduced French vanilla yogurt
	Fresh mint leaves for garnish (optional)

Use local apples in this recipe. Since we are the OHEA, we naturally used Ontario apples. Here we chose Red Delicious for their firmness, but for a softer apple, choose a Honeycrisp or Ambrosia.

1. Prepare Basic Quinoa Crêpes (page 171). When the crêpes are made, in a large frying pan over medium heat, add the non-hydrogenated margarine and sauté the apple slices for 2 to 3 minutes, until they start to become translucent.

2. Add the brown sugar, stirring to coat fruit, and cook for about 2 to 4 minutes, until the mixture is just starting to bubble.

3. Add the spices and continue to simmer for 5 to 10 minutes, or until the apple slices are tender but not mushy. (Recipe can be made in advance to this point. Cool, refrigerate and then reheat just before serving.)

4. **TO ASSEMBLE:** To make sure each crêpe is flavour enhanced, working quickly, brush each crêpe with some of the cooked apple mixture. Fold the crêpes in quarters and place two crêpes on each of six plates. Spoon one-sixth of the apple mixture overtop each pair of crêpes. Add ¼ cup (60 mL) of yogurt to each serving and sprinkle with cinnamon. Drizzle any remaining sauce over the crêpes.

5. **TO SERVE:** Garnish with mint if desired. Serve immediately. For a special fall dessert, 2 Tbsp (30 mL) of rum can be stirred into the apple mixture after it has been taken off the heat. Finish the presentation as described in Step 4.

Makes 12 crêpes • One serving = 2 crêpes with ⅙ of the cooked apple mixture and ¼ cup (60 mL) of yogurt

Nutrition per serving

373 calories	18 g total fat	3 g saturated fat
39 mg cholesterol	74 mg sodium	49 g carbohydrates
3 g fibre	34 g sugars	7 g protein

Excellent source of vitamin D.

SUMMER

Joan Ttooulias, PHEc

Just to be a rabble-rouser—here is a quinoa pudding that is served in the summer, when local berries are in season. From the milk, quinoa and almonds, this dessert has enough protein that you could add it to your breakfast or lunch menu. Talk about having your pudding and eating it too.

Pudding with Roasted Berries

BERRIES

1 lb (500 g)	strawberries, hulled and halved
6 oz (175 g)	raspberries
½ tsp (2 mL)	cinnamon

PUDDING

1 cup (250 mL)	quinoa, rinsed and drained
2½ cups (625 mL)	skim milk, divided
2 Tbsp (30 mL)	honey
1 Tbsp (15 mL)	cornstarch
½ cup (125 mL)	whole almonds, coarsely chopped

To vary the taste of this versatile dessert, when in season, try using roasted peaches, roasted rhubarb sweetened with 3 Tbsp (45 mL) of honey, roasted plums or a mixture of roasted apples, pears and apricots.

1. **BERRIES:** Preheat the oven to 325°F (160°C). Line a 9- × 13-inch (3.5 L) metal baking pan with parchment paper. Place the berries on the paper, sprinkle with cinnamon, and roast in the centre of the oven for 45 minutes.

2. **PUDDING:** Meanwhile, place the quinoa in a large saucepan, add 2 cups (500 mL) of the milk and the honey. Bring to a boil, then reduce heat to medium-low and cook covered for 18 to 20 minutes, stirring often to avoiding scorching.

3. Whisk together the remaining ½ cup (125 mL) of milk and the cornstarch until mixture is smooth. Add to the cooked quinoa mixture in the saucepan and return to a boil. Cook, stirring continuously, until the mixture is bubbling and has thickened.

4. Stir in the almonds, cover and remove from heat. Let sit for 10 minutes.

5. **TO SERVE:** Ever so gently, fold in the roasted berries. Spoon into serving bowls. Or, for a different look, serve the pudding as is and top each serving with one-sixth of the berries.

Makes 3 cups (750 mL) • One serving = ½ cup (125 mL) pudding with ⅓ cup (80 mL) roasted berries

Nutrition per serving

277 calories	8 g total fat	1 g saturated fat
2 mg cholesterol	53 mg sodium	43 g carbohydrates
7 g fibre	16 g sugars	11 g protein

Excellent source of vitamin C, magnesium and iron.

In the heat of the summer, make this light dessert in the microwave to keep your kitchen cool and your hydro bill cooler.

YEAR ROUND

Cindy Fendall, PHEc

Orange-Scented Quinoa with Blueberries

1. In an 8-cup (2 L) round, preferably deep microwave dish, combine the quinoa, orange juice and water. Cover and microwave at High (100%) for 5 minutes to bring to a boil, then at 60% for 8 to 12 minutes, or until the liquid has been absorbed.

2. Fluff with a fork and let stand covered for 5 minutes. Stir in the blueberries, cover and let sit for 5 minutes. Cool completely in the fridge.

3. **TO SERVE:** Fold in the mint, divide the pudding equally between 4 dessert bowls and sprinkle with nuts if desired.

Makes about 2 cups (500 mL) • One serving = ½ cup (125 mL)

½ cup (125 mL)	quinoa, rinsed and drained
¾ cup (185 mL)	orange juice
3 Tbsp (45 mL)	water
¾ cup (185 mL)	fresh blueberries
¼ cup (60 mL)	fresh mint, chiffonade (see page 8)
¼ cup (60 mL)	whole almonds, coarsely chopped, for garnish (optional)

Nutrition per serving

93 calories	0 g total fat	0 g saturated fat
0 mg cholesterol	7 mg sodium	20 g carbohydrates
1 g fibre	12 g sugars	2 g protein

Excellent source of vitamin C.

This elegant, moist and flavourful cake is a perfect dessert for a fall family dinner. Serve warm with a dollop of vanilla yogurt and a sprinkle of icing sugar, and suddenly you have a dessert to serve to company. It's all in the presentation.

Honey Spiced Pear Cake

PEARS

¼ cup (60 mL)	liquid honey
1 Tbsp (15 mL)	fresh lemon juice
¼ tsp (1 mL)	ground cardamom
¼ tsp (1 mL)	cinnamon
¼ tsp (1 mL)	ground ginger
4	ripe pears, peeled (optional), cored and quartered lengthwise

BATTER

½ cup (125 mL)	non-hydrogenated margarine
½ cup (125 mL)	granulated sugar
2	omega-3 eggs
¾ cup (185 mL)	whole wheat flour
½ cup (125 mL)	quinoa flour (see page 7)
1 tsp (5 mL)	baking powder
1 tsp (5 mL)	cinnamon
½ tsp (2 mL)	ground cardamom
½ tsp (2 mL)	ground ginger
½ cup (125 mL)	1% milk

1. Preheat the oven to 350°F (175°C). Insert a round piece of parchment in the bottom of a 10-inch (25 cm) springform pan and lightly grease the sides with canola oil. Wrapping the outside of the cake pan with foil helps to prevent any honey from leaking out and scorching during baking.

2. **PEARS:** In a small saucepan over low heat, gently combine the honey with the lemon, cardamom, cinnamon and ginger. Meanwhile, arrange the pears, cut side down, decoratively in the bottom of the prepared cake pan. Drizzle evenly with the honey mixture. Set aside.

3. **BATTER:** In a large bowl, using an electric mixer, beat the margarine with the sugar until fluffy. Beat in the eggs one at a time until fluffy.

4. In a separate bowl, whisk together the whole wheat flour and quinoa flours, baking powder, cinnamon, cardamom and ginger. Add half of the dry mixture to the margarine and eggs and stir in, then add half of the milk to the batter and stir in. Repeat—flour, stir in, milk, stir in. Beat until smooth and combined. Do not overmix.

5. Spread the batter evenly over the pear mixture. Bake in the centre of the oven for 60 to 75 minutes, or until a toothpick inserted in the centre comes out clean.

6. **TO SERVE:** Cool for 5 minutes and turn out onto a serving platter. Serve warm or let cool to room temperature.

Makes 12 servings • One serving = ¹⁄₁₂ wedge of cake

Nutrition per serving

236 calories	10 g total fat	2 g saturated fat
33 mg cholesterol	18 mg sodium	36 g carbohydrates
3 g fibre	26 g sugars	3 g protein

Excellent source of vitamin D.

A spin on a classic 1930s dish, this rich and chocolatey pudding cake is an easy dessert to make for your family. As an even bigger treat, serve it warm with a scoop of frozen vanilla yogurt.

FALL and **WINTER**

Amy Snider-Whitson, PHEc

Rich Chocolate Pudding Cake

1. Preheat the oven to 350°F (175°C). Lightly grease an 8-inch (20 cm) square metal baking pan with canola oil.

2. **CAKE BATTER:** In a medium bowl, whisk together the flour, sugar, cocoa powder and baking powder until well combined.

3. In a separate bowl, whisk together the milk, egg and oil.

4. Whisk the wet ingredients into the dry ingredients just until combined. Spread evenly into the prepared pan.

5. **TOPPING:** In a medium bowl, whisk the boiling water with the sugar, cocoa powder and espresso or coffee.

6. Pour the topping carefully and evenly over the batter. Bake for 22 to 24 minutes, or until the cake bounces back when lightly touched. Remove from the oven.

7. **TO SERVE:** There will be sauce in the pan. Scoop out a portion of the cake and spoon sauce over top. Best if served warm.

Makes 8 servings • One serving = about 1⅓ cups (330 mL)

CAKE BATTER	
¾ cup (185 mL)	quinoa flour (see page 7)
⅓ cup (80 mL)	granulated sugar
2 Tbsp (30 mL)	natural unsweetened cocoa powder, sifted if lumpy (see sidebar page 154)
1 tsp (5 mL)	baking powder
⅓ cup (80 mL)	skim milk or organic unsweetened fortified soy beverage
1	omega-3 egg
2 Tbsp (30 mL)	canola oil
TOPPING	
1⅓ cups (330 mL)	boiling water
1 cup (250 mL)	brown sugar, packed
⅓ cup (80 mL)	natural cocoa powder, sifted if lumpy
2 tsp (10 mL)	instant espresso or coffee granules

Nutrition per serving

235 calories	5 g total fat	1 g saturated fat
25 mg cholesterol	63 mg sodium	46 g carbohydrates
3 g fibre	35 g sugars	4 g protein

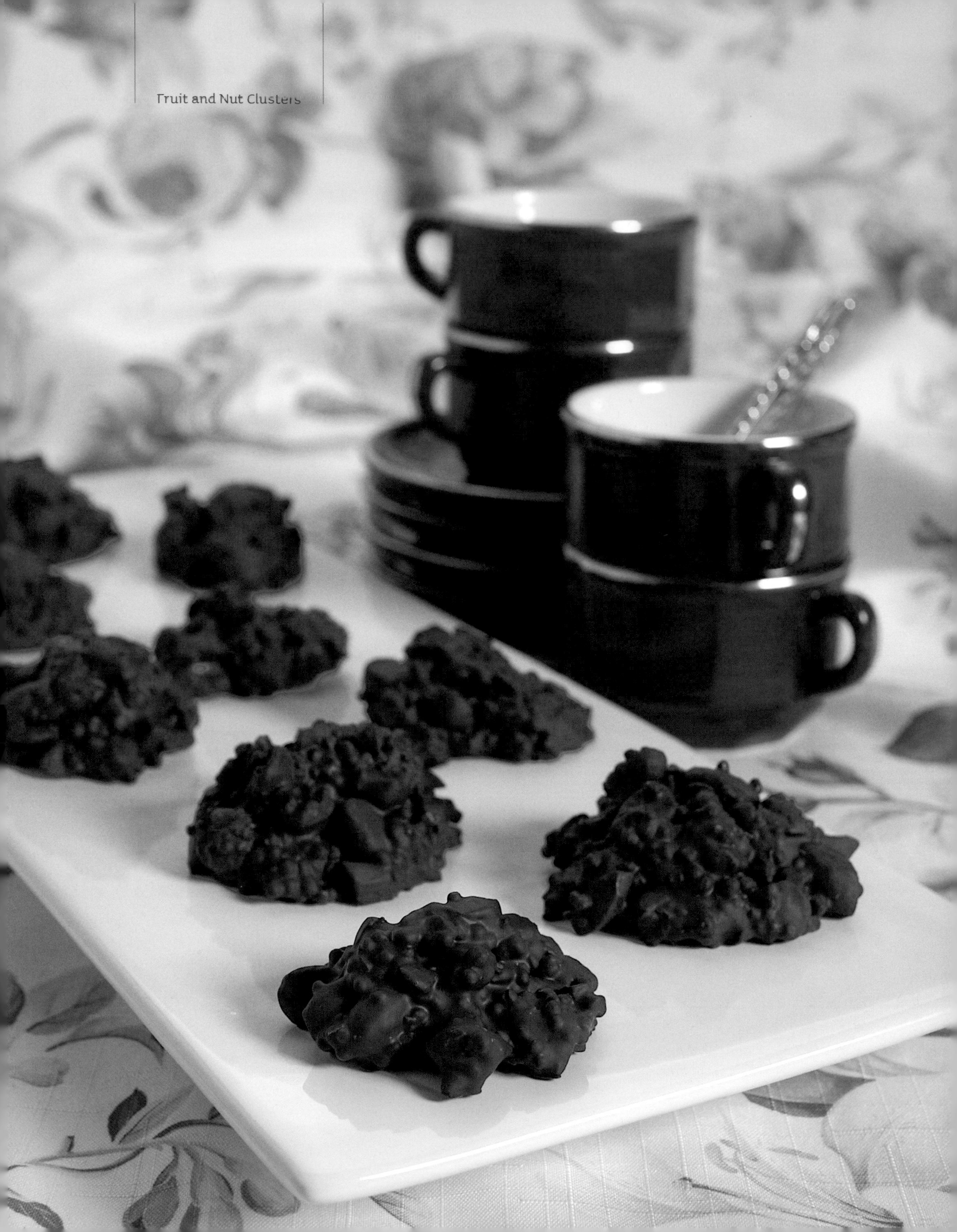

Fruit and Nut Clusters

Some dinner parties just call for *one* decadent treat as the dessert. This is *that* dessert. Serve with tea or coffee and your company will rave. NOTE: You can find quinoa puffs in the cereal aisle in most high-end grocery stores or at a health food store.

YEAR ROUND

Cathy Ireland, PHEc

Fruit and Nut Clusters

6 oz (175 g)	bittersweet chocolate, coarsely chopped, 70%–75% cocoa mass
½ cup (125 mL)	quinoa puffs (see page 7)
½ cup (125 mL)	dried cranberries
½ cup (125 mL)	whole almonds, coarsely chopped

1. Line a large baking sheet (11- × 17-inch/28 × 42 cm) with parchment paper and set aside. Place the chocolate in a medium microwave-safe bowl. Microwave at Medium for 1 minute, stir, microwave one more minute at Medium and stir again until completely melted. Depending on your wattage, this could take longer than 2 minutes. The trick is to add more time in 5-second intervals, as you don't want to scorch the chocolate. Stir until the chocolate has completely melted.

2. Add the quinoa puffs, cranberries and almonds. Stir to combine.

3. Drop 12 equal spoonfuls of the chocolate mixture on the prepared baking sheet.

4. Let set until firm, about 30 minutes, or refrigerate until firm. Store in the fridge in an airtight container. Serve at room temperature.

Makes 12 clusters • One serving = 1 cluster

Nutrition per serving

134 calories	9 g total fat	3 g saturated fat
0 mg cholesterol	0 mg sodium	15 g carbohydrates
2 g fibre	9 g sugars	3 g protein

Acknowledgements

WE ARE MANY AND SO THERE ARE MANY TO THANK. First of all, a round of applause goes to Michael Burch, CEO of Whitecap, who came up with the brilliant idea for this cookbook. He's the one who planted the seed (as it were). Warmest thanks also to the board, executive and members of the Ontario Home Economics Association (OHEA), who made this book possible by providing creative recipes and encouragement throughout the process. In particular, I am grateful to Amy Snider-Whitson, PHEc, who jumped on board at the outset and not only did all of the nutrient breakdowns, but also submitted recipes and was the go-to person from start to finish.

I also thank Barb Holland, PHEc, for helping with some of the reformatting of the recipes and especially for sitting in my dining room one Friday morning and methodically double-checking to make sure all those who submitted recipes were included in the contributors list. Big thanks to her for the pictures of quinoa growing in Peru. As fate had it, she was in Peru while this book was in the works. Serendipity? I think so.

Thank you as well to the Ryerson students who slogged through winter weather over to my wee kitchen in Toronto to test recipes almost elbow to elbow:

Shoshana Akselro

Jodi Bernstein

Nusaiba Bhoola

Katie Brunke

Katie Cvitkovitch

Oksana Dovganyk

Lily Fatemi

Spencer Finch-
   Coursey

Paula Gilchrist

Joseph Horvath

Lauren Kennedy

Nida Khan

Michelle Kwan

Eileen Mendoza

Iana Mologuina

Martin Moraleja

Antonia Morganti

Angela Pavarin-
   De Luca

Nazima Qureshi

Kate Sinclair

Izabela Smolik

Lisa Snider-Nevin

Maysa Tani

Emilie Trottier

Nicole Turner

Katherine Vanker

Alissa Vieth

Right: Some of the book's recipe contributors and testers

Opposite: Quinoa growing in Peru (photo by Barb Holland)

Those 16 days in December were a learning experience for all of us! I personally had many great laughs, although the time the kitchen was nearly blown up was a tad scary. Thanks to the power of baking soda, even the burnt pots turned out as good as new. I might just be insane enough to want to do this again. Might . . .

Thank you to Erin MacGregor, Registered Dietician and PHEc, for checking that the nutrition facts were perfect, and to Nancy Greiter, OHEA's administrator, for her tremendous help in organizing emails, sending me this and that and reminding me what the password was for the email account when I was having a brain cramp. I am grateful also to Joan Ttooulias, PHEc, for fabulous food styling and her amazing sense of humour, and to Mike McColl for his perfect photos and his wonderful patience. Together they were a winning team. Heartfelt appreciation also to Cindy Fendall, PHEc, who was an amazing part of the photo shoot team for three of the five days; Andrea Villneff for her help and the left-handed hand modelling for the how-tos; Astrid Muschalla, PHEc, for her help and for doing a day's worth of grocery shopping to boot; Michele McAdoo, PHEc, and

Barb Holland, PHEc, for their spectacular help and organizational skills and the laughs on the last day of the shoot, by which time both Joan and I had forgotten most of the nouns in the English language. And where would a cookbook editor be without dishwashers, dish dryers, choppers and general helpers? Lost! So a special thanks to students Spencer Finch-Coursey, Joseph Horvath, Alissa Vieth, Katie Brunke, Nazima Qureshi and Nida Khan for the photo shoot help. Special thanks for Donna Washburn, PHEc, and Heather Butt, PHEc, for going through the recipes to determine which ones were gluten free ⬤. Special thanks to Marion Kane for the lifetime loan of the amazing bowl pictured on page 110. Thanks to Joan Ttooulias and Michelle Kwan for helping with the proofreading.

To Michelle Furbacher, the art director at Whitecap, thanks for her patience and all of the great creative input. Thanks to Theresa Best, also at Whitecap, for her support, phone calls and suggestions, and for talking me through the editing process. To Naomi Pauls for her amazing edit, clear thinking and eagle eye. And to everyone else at Whitecap who made this book sing!

Contributors

JANET BUIS, PHEc, graduated from Brescia University College at the University of Western Ontario in 1989. She works as a monasterian cook at the Sisters in the Precious Blood Monastery in London, Ontario, where she enjoys the challenge of preparing creative and nutritious meals for a diversity of Sisters and retreatants from around the world.

JANET BUTTERS, PHEc, has held her Professional Home Economist designation for the past ten years. She is married and has a teenage son heading to university. Janet promotes the science of smart living every day— both in her human resources role in the public sector and in her many roles at home.

DEB CAMPBELL, PHEc, has been practising professional home economics for 40 years primarily in education. She taught at Brescia College in London, Ontario, and Centralia College until its closure in 1994. Deb now practises as a freelance home economist, after almost 15 years with Ontario Pork as a field rep working with consumers.

EMILY CAMPBELL, SHEA STUDENT MEMBER, holds a BA in the sociology of health and aging. She is currently pursuing a second degree at Brescia University College, an honours specialization Bachelor of Science in nutrition and dietetics. Emily is also actively involved in the Alpha Phi International Women's Fraternity.

MARY CARVER, PHEc, is an Ottawa-based former teacher who taught at Frontenac Secondary School, Kingston; Centre Wellington High School, Fergus; Madame Vanier Children's Services, London; and Kemptville College at the University of Guelph. She is the OHEA public relations coordinator.

JOAN CHATFIELD, OHEA CORRESPONDING MEMBER, is a part-time bilingual customer service representative. She loves to cook for her family and enjoys adapting recipes to suit her needs. As a busy mother of two boys, she often seeks out easy recipes that are nutritious and can be served again for either lunch or dinner the next day.

LAURA CRAIG, PHEc, left the teaching profession to follow her love for food by becoming a Professional Home Economist and dietician. She is currently undertaking an internship in dietetics. Laura loves to cook and alter recipes, and she hopes to write her own cookbook.

MARGARET DICKENSON, PHEc, is a cookbook author and TV host. Her self-published recipe book *Margaret's Table* was chosen Best of the Best Cookbook in the entertaining category at the Gourmand World Cookbook Awards. In 2010, *Ottawa Life* magazine recognized Margaret as one of the "Top 50 People in the Capital."

SUSAN DONALDSON, PHEc, trained as a home economist in England. When working in South Africa, she learned to love Cajun food from a colleague from Baton Rouge, Louisiana. Since then Susan has sailed across oceans and gathered recipes from many different cultures.

STEVE DUBÉ, SHEA STUDENT MEMBER, is enrolled in the nutrition program at Brescia University College and is an expert in physical fitness. He values health, happiness and the pleasures of eating with loved ones.

MARLENE DYER, PHEc, graduated from Ryerson University with a degree in foods and nutrition. She is a food technologist specializing in recipe product development. The opportunity to contribute to this cookbook allowed her to combine two of her favourite desserts, oatmeal cookies and brownies, into a tasty, better-for-you snack option.

CHANTELLE ELSON, SHEA STUDENT MEMBER, is a foods and nutrition student at Brescia University College, aiming to become a dietician. Her first degree was in kinesiology, so she is always trying to create recipes to help optimize that training. Chantelle loves to cook and bake and is constantly altering recipes to make them healthier and still delicious.

ROCHELLE ETHIER, OHEA STUDENT MEMBER, is a graduate of the Brescia University College dietetics program. Her goal is to keep our planet healthy, and her passion for food runs deep. For Rochelle, living with type 1 diabetes is an exciting opportunity to strive for optimal health.

CINDY FENDALL, PHEc, is a graduate of the nutrition and food science program at the University of Alberta. Her role as a home economist is engaging communities to be competent in making healthful food choices for their families and developing sustainable food policies and an accountable food industry.

CRISTINA FERNANDES, PHEc, is also a registered dietician. She has tremendous faith in the power of food and finds great joy in helping others help themselves reach and maintain a desired level of health through nutrition, while enjoying every bite.

CAROLYN FRAIL, PHEc, has been a Professional Home Economist since 2004. She is a freelance food and nutrition writer and a fitness enthusiast. Carolyn enjoys cooking healthy meals for her family and friends and creating delicious lunches that her kids (she hopes) will not trade at school.

HEIKE BEATRIX HEINZE, PHEc, specializes in food, nutrition and health. Her areas of expertise include organic and vegetarian food and sustainable eating. Heike has been working as an educator, consultant, researcher and writer. She has been a vegetarian for over 25 years and is an active member of Canadian Organic Growers Toronto.

WENDI HIEBERT, PHEc, is a freelance home economist, food writer and educator. She develops and edits recipes and gives "Sip, Savour and Smile" culinary talks and dining etiquette presentations. She knows lots about eggs and loves chocolate, afternoon tea, live theatre and her poodle, Cocoa.

JENNIFER HILL, PHEc, is also an Ontario certified teacher. She works as a daily occasional teacher, patiently awaiting the day when she can have her own Family Studies classroom. Jennifer also works at a local homeless shelter and loves creating recipes that fit within her gluten-free dietary restrictions.

JOYCE HO, OHEA STUDENT MEMBER, is a foods and nutrition student and an eager at-home cook and baker. Experimenting with everyday foods or different cultural ingredients is a path she would like to pursue in the future. Her appetite for delicious food is insatiable.

BARB HOLLAND, PHEc, is a Professional Home Economist who does recipe development, media appearances and cooking demonstrations. Barb has worked behind and in front of the camera in many a TV studio—as a food stylist and spokesperson. She is a fitness enthusiast who enjoys running, cycling and curling.

ERICA HORNER, SHEA STUDENT MEMBER, is working toward her second undergraduate degree, finally following her passion, food. She has spent the majority of her life living a healthy, active lifestyle and has always enjoyed modifying recipes to make them healthier.

GABRIELE HOSSBACH, PHEc, spent the greater part of her working life in an institutional food services environment. Her love for her husband, an insulin-dependent diabetic, and the availability of a little more time have enabled her to channel her passion for food and her nutrition knowledge into healthy recipes.

HEATHER HOWE, PHEc, has 22 years' experience in the food industry. She worked for over twenty years in the *Canadian Living* magazine test kitchen and currently works as a freelance home economist developing and testing recipes, writing about food, doing nutritional counselling and teaching sewing classes.

CATHY IRELAND, PHEc, has been a Professional Home Economist at Kraft since 1995. She began her career in Food Service, developing menus for restaurants and supporting the Coffee division, perfecting the art of tasting coffee. Although Cathy has worked with every Kraft product, each day brings new experiences.

PATRICIA JEFKINS-SMITH, PHEc, is a retired Family Studies teacher from the Hamilton area. She is no stranger to adapting recipes to meet the needs of gluten-free and vegetarian diets in her family. Her dinner table is always open to guests, and she loves to sew, bake, downhill ski and travel.

OLGA KAMINSKYJ, PHEc, considers herself fortunate to have a career in food, which is also her lifelong passion. As a food stylist and recipe developer, she gets to play with her food and eat it too!

FALGUNI KAPADIA, PHEc, is a community nutrition educator with Toronto Public Health. Falguni works with diverse communities. She assists parents of young children in improving their food-selecting, -purchasing and -preparing skills in a group setting. Falguni develops and alters recipes to make them healthier and culturally specific.

LAURA KATZ, SHEA STUDENT MEMBER, is a student at the University of Western Ontario and an aspiring food scientist and chef. Laura gets her cooking inspiration from Ina Garten, the "Barefoot Contessa," and Martha Stewart. When she is not studying in the library, she is coming up with new recipes and ideas in the kitchen.

LINDA LICHTENBERGER, PHEc, says that if she were a food, her current label would include "Granny L." While she began university as a "Mac" girl at Guelph, she graduated from "FACS" as the program evolved. Regarding food choices, her mother called her a "purist," so cooking with quinoa suits her perfectly.

ERIN MACGREGOR, PHEc, is a registered dietitian and a bona fide food lover. By day, Erin works as a dietitian in a large urban hospital and is an active member of the OHEA board of directors. By night, she loves to relax by perusing her favourite food and food photography blogs and cooking for friends and family.

JENNIFER MACKENZIE, PHEc, is a freelance food writer, a recipe developer and editor, a media spokesperson and the author of five cookbooks, including the bestselling *Complete Book of Pickling* (Robert Rose, 2009). Jennifer co-owns Nuttshell Next Door café in Lakefield, Ontario, with her husband, chef Jay Nutt.

JAN MAIN, PHEc, has been teaching, catering and writing about food for over 30 years. She is the author of four cookbooks, including *200 Best Lactose-Free Recipes* (Firefly Books, 2006) and *The Best Freezer Cookbook* (Robert Rose, 2008). Currently, she is a culinary arts teacher who loves to inspire others with her love of food.

TERESA MAKAREWICZ, PHEc, was the driving force behind the first Canadian in-house cooking school in a grocery store. Currently, she freelances, representing clients as a spokesperson, food stylist and recipe developer and tester. Teresa loves to share her passion for healthy food ideas and anything "foodie."

MICHELE MCADOO, PHEc, has worked for 16 years in the Kraft Kitchens. Michele developed a strong appreciation of food while growing up on a beef farm. She is a graduate of Ryerson University and an active member in OHEA and OHEIB. Michele passionately enjoys eating her way around the world.

ASTRID MUSCHALLA, PHEc, is a Red Seal Cook, food and nutrition educator and organic horticulture specialist. Her company, Oasis Institute for Healthy Living Inc., is involved with many national public and private organizations to bring healthy living education to individuals, families and communities.

MARLA NICHOLLS, PHEc, is a retired Family Studies teacher who enjoyed teaching others the practicality and love of food preparation for 35 years. She delights in transforming a meal from standard to stupendous. Her love for textiles and fashion continues in creating figure skating costumes, custom clothing and embroidery.

DIANE O'SHEA, PHEc, loves food! As a Family Studies educator and advocate for agrifood education, she is able to share her passion with students at both secondary and university levels.

NAZIMA QURESHI, OHEA STUDENT MEMBER, is in the nutrition and food program at Ryerson University. She spends most of her time involved in activities that enrich her experience as a nutrition student. During her free time, Nazima experiments with new recipes and perfects her cake decorating skills.

BAILEY RAFFERTY, SHEA STUDENT MEMBER, is enrolled in the nutrition and dietetics program at Brescia University College. She cooks as a hobby and often invites friends to try some dish she has concocted. Bailey says she rarely follows recipes exactly, improvising often and substituting whatever she has on hand.

LINDA REASBECK, PHEc, is a retired educator and entrepreneur. Her main career was in the Food Science and Technology Section at Kemptville College. After retiring early, she owned and operated a gift store called Saffron's in Manotick, Ontario. Currently she volunteers on several community boards and loves spending time with a new granddaughter.

EMILY RICHARDS, PHEc, has authored and co-authored many cookbooks and continues to create recipes for notable magazines, newspapers and companies. Emily appears across the country presenting recipes and easy cooking and entertaining ideas, always promoting her passion for food and inspiring people to get in their kitchens and cook.

DIANA RODEL, PHEc, relishes creating meals that are nutrient-rich and varied in colour, texture and tastes. She uses her menu-planning skills in working as a dietetic technician, volunteering as the nutritional/menu consultant with a community after-school program, and preparing everyday meal ideas.

ANNA SHIER, OHEA STUDENT MEMBER, is a graduate student at Brescia University College studying to be a registered dietitian. She loves to cook and decided early in her career that she wanted to integrate culinary skills into dietetic practice. As a result, she has completed culinary training and is excited to combine the culinary arts with the nutritional sciences.

ELAINE SILVERTHORN, PHEc, is a semi-retired Family Studies teacher from Ottawa. She started teaching the baby boomers when they reached high school age, and she now has a home-based business focused on healthy anti-aging to meet the needs of baby boomers as they become middle-aged.

MAIRLYN SMITH, PHEc, is an award-winning cookbook author and TV cook. She is a regular guest expert on CityLine and a familiar face on BT Toronto. Her previous book, *Healthy Starts Here!*, is helping to further her dream that all Canadians jump on the health train *tout de suite*!

AMY SNIDER-WHITSON, PHEc, is a food writer, recipe developer, media spokesperson and culinary nutrition consultant. As president of The Test Kitchen Inc., Amy uses her skills to develop hundreds of recipes for recognized food brands each year. She enjoys combining her love of cooking with her understanding of healthy eating.

SUSANNE STARK, PHEc, leads the What's Cooking development and Ethnic program in the Kraft Kitchens. Susanne has worked as a home economist for over 20 years. She started her career developing recipes as a freelance home economist in Toronto and later joined Kraft Canada, where she has worked since 1997.

ROSEMARIE SUPERVILLE, PHEc, is a Toronto home economist specializing in food styling, recipe development and food and travel writing. Food and travel are her passions, and she enjoys writing about both. Rosemarie food-styles for print advertising, packaging and magazines; she often creates recipes for clients and then turns them into mouth-watering pictures.

ELLIE TOPP, PHEc, is a certified culinary professional with a master's degree in foods and nutrition. She has authored nine cookbooks, including *Fresh and Healthy Cooking for Two* (with Marilyn Booth, Formac, 2011) and *The Complete Book of Small-Batch Preserving* (with Margaret Howard, Firefly Books, 2007). Her research on flavoured oils was published in *Food Research International*.

OLGA TRUCHAN, PHEc, has been a food stylist in Toronto for over 35 years. She has worked with many food companies, magazines, marketing boards, restaurateurs and chefs in Canada and the United States. She loves good food, cooking, eating and drinking wine.

JOAN TTOOULIAS, PHEc, is a practising home economist who emigrated from England. Joan worked for a major food company, then started her own business styling food for commercials, packaging and print and developing recipes for companies and publications. She is a passionate advocate for Home Economics, in whatever guise, being taught in every school.

ROSEMARY VANDERHOEVEN, PHEc, teaches Family Studies to adult high school students. Her background is in clothing, textiles and personal finance. Rosemary enjoys cooking and baking for her family.

ANDREA VILLNEFF, OHEA PROVISIONAL MEMBER, is a 2011 graduate of the University of Guelph and currently works as a home economist. Her favourite pastimes include travelling, running and spending time with friends and family. Her passion for nutrition and the culinary arts has shown her how food can be both nutritious and delicious.

GRACE WARMELS, SHEA STUDENT MEMBER, has a fondness for cooking that began back when her only job was to stir the ingredients for her mother. Her other passions now include team sports, travel and yoga.

DONNA WASHBURN, PHEc, & HEATHER BUTT, PHEc, met while college professors in foods and nutrition and together began Quality Professional Services. They developed wheat- and gluten-free recipes for bread machine manufacturers and operated call centres for a yeast company and appliance manufacturers. Presently working on a seventh gluten-free cookbook, they have co-created both Canadian and American wheat versions of *300 Bread Machine Recipes*. As best-selling authors they enjoy the challenge of developing flavourful and nutritious gluten-free recipes in their test kitchen.

MARNIE WEBB, PHEc, graduated with a degree in human nutrition from the University of Guelph. Marnie currently works for the Ontario Ministry of Agriculture, Food and Rural Affairs and lives in Guelph. As a busy mother of two teenagers, she enjoys trying easy, nutritious recipes.

BRIDGET WILSON, PHEc, is a freelance consulting home economist in the Toronto area who specializes in recipe development and project management. She is passionate about creating delicious and healthy recipes that consumers will enjoy.

Online Resources

Quinoa growing in Peru (photo by Barb Holland)

Alberta Human Ecology and Home Economics
Association (AHEA)
www.ahea.ab.ca

Canada's Food Guide
www.hc-sc.gc.ca/fn-an/food-guide-aliment/
index-eng.php

Canadian Celiac Association
www.celiac.ca/diet.php

Canadian Home Economics Foundation (CHEF)
www.chef-fcef.ca

Manitoba Association of Home Economists (MAHE)
www.homefamily.net

Ontario Home Economics Association (OHEA)
www.ohea.on.ca

Ontario Home Economists in Business (OHEIB)
www.oheib.org

Students' Human Ecology Association (SHEA)
www.brescia-shea.ca

Whole Grains Council
www.wholegrainscouncil.org

Index